THE FOLGER LIBRARY SHAKESPEARE

Designed to make Shakespeare's classic plays available to the general reader, each edition contains a reliable text with modernized spelling and punctuation, scene-by-scene plot summaries, and explanatory notes clarifying obscure and obsolete expressions. An interpretive essay and accounts of Shakespeare's life and theater form an instructive preface to each play.

Louis B. Wright, General Editor, was the Director of the Folger Shakespeare Library from 1948 until his retirement in 1968. He is the author of *Middle-Class Culture in Elizabethan England, Religion and Empire, Shakespeare for Everyman,* and many other books and essays on the history and literature of the Tudor and Stuart periods.

Virginia Lamar, Assistant Editor, served as research assistant to the Director and Executive Secretary of the Folger Shakespeare Library from 1946 until her death in 1968. She is the author of *English Dress in the Age of Shakespeare* and *Travel and Roads in England,* and coeditor of William Strachey's *Historie of Travell into Virginia Britania.*

The Folger Shakespeare Library

The Folger Shakespeare Library in Washington, D.C., a research institute founded and endowed by Henry Clay Folger and administered by the Trustees of Amherst College, contains the world's largest collection of Shakespeareana. Although the Folger Library's primary purpose is to encourage advanced research in history and literature, it has continually exhibited a profound concern in stimulating a popular interest in the Elizabethan period.

GENERAL EDITOR

LOUIS B. WRIGHT

Director, Folger Shakespeare Library, 1948–1968

ASSISTANT EDITOR

VIRGINIA A. LaMAR

Executive Secretary, Folger Shakespeare Library, 1946–1968

The Folger Library General Reader's Shakespeare

AS YOU LIKE IT

by

WILLIAM SHAKESPEARE

WASHINGTON SQUARE PRESS
PUBLISHED BY POCKET BOOKS

New York   London   Toronto   Sydney   Tokyo   Singapore

A Washington Square Press Publication of
POCKET BOOKS, a division of Simon & Schuster Inc.
1230 Avenue of the Americas, New York, NY 10020

ISBN: 0-671-72953-5

First Pocket Books printing January 1960

33   32   31   30   29   28

WASHINGTON SQUARE PRESS and WSP colophon are
registered trademarks of Simon & Schuster Inc.

Printed in the U.S.A.

Preface

This edition of *As You Like It* is designed to make available a readable text of one of Shakespeare's most popular plays. In the centuries since Shakespeare many changes have occurred in the meanings of words, and some clarification of Shakespeare's vocabulary may be helpful. To provide the reader with necessary notes in the most accessible format, we have placed them on the pages facing the text that they explain. We have tried to make these notes as brief and simple as possible. Preliminary to the text we have also included a brief statement of essential information about Shakespeare and his stage. Readers desiring more detailed information should refer to the books suggested in the references, and if still further information is needed, the bibliographies in those books will provide the necessary clues to the literature of the subject.

The early texts of all of Shakespeare's plays provide only inadequate stage directions, and it is conventional for modern editors to add many that clarify the action. Such additions, and additions to entrances, are placed in square brackets.

All illustrations are from material in the Folger Library collections.

L. B. W.
V. A. L.

June 15, 1959

Woodland Magic

As You Like It appeals to the perennial love of the English-speaking peoples for the open country, for the glades and woods of a country perpetually green. On every holiday the towns and cities of England empty as the inhabitants stream outward in search of greenswards, meadows, parks, and forest paths. For the city dweller a touch of nature at Whitsuntide or on August bank holiday means a return to quiet and sanity not to be found in the roar of cities. Shakespeare's Englishmen were as appreciative as their descendants of the countryside, and Shakespeare wrote into *As You Like It* his own poetic tribute to the attractions of the woodlands of Warwickshire. For the Forest of Arden, where he set the play, is Warwickshire, however many olive trees and lionesses the players might discover therein.

In the prose romances of chivalric adventure, the settings were usually in some unreal land of Arcady where one found lovelorn maidens in the company of shepherds and shepherdesses. The forests most likely were inhabited by giants, dwarfs, hermits, and enchantresses, not to mention troublesome or strange fauna that included dragons, cockatrices, and an occasional unicorn. Although Shakespeare took his story from a popular romance, he managed to domesticate his setting, and, as absurd as the plot is, one somehow feels that the scenery is not far from something he has seen and experienced. To the Londoner who saw the play at the Globe, it must have smelled of the woods to the north of the city on a May day.

As Shakespeare sat in his London lodgings writing these swift-moving lines, his mind was far away in the woodlands north of the Avon, which bore the name of Arden. Scholars have learnedly argued that the setting is clearly in some French duchy and it must be in the Ardennes near the Flanders border. Whatever may be the nominal location, and whatever incongruities remain from the romance that was the source of the play, the atmosphere is that of the English countryside.

Shakespeare himself, like most Englishmen of the time, was not far removed from the country. Stratford-upon-Avon, then a country town of about two thousand people, nestles in one of the most beautiful counties of England, a well-watered land of forests, farms, and sheep pastures. The sheepcote that Rosalind set out to buy could have been a stone's throw from Shakespeare's father's farm at Snitterfield. Shakespeare always displayed the common sense and balance that one frequently finds in men brought up in the country, and in *As You Like It* he exhibits in marked degree qualities that indicate a man in harmony with nature.

The theme of the play is love in various aspects, but Shakespeare never lets his treatment of the subject drift into absurdity, as so often happened in the romances. He can laugh gaily and happily at the perplexities that love can bring, but he is neither sentimental nor cynical. Even Rosalind in love is able to display a sense of humor about love and lovers, including herself. In this play, Shakespeare is not concerned with profound overtones and cosmic truths. He is writing a play of merriment and good humor, and audiences have liked it from his day until our own.

Shakespeare derived the plot and most of the incidents in *As You Like It* from a prose romance, a short novel by Thomas Lodge entitled *Rosalynde, or Euphues' Golden Legacy* (1590). Lodge, writing in the elaborate and somewhat artificial "euphuistic" manner popular at the time, told his tale in a high and serious style without any humor. Fantastic romances were popular in the Elizabethan period and no one asked for verisimilitude. Some of these romances, in cheap editions, delighted apprentices and others besides. Everyone knew about *Palmerin of England, Amadis of Gaul,* and a score of other chivalric romances of the kind that were the undoing of Cervantes' knight, Don Quixote. Like Cervantes, Shakespeare could utilize the themes of romance for gently satiric purposes, and in *As You Like It* he introduces characters that would have jarred in Lodge's story. Shakespeare's additions include the comic parts of Touchstone and Audrey, William, and Jaques. Someone has observed that Touchstone serves as a foil to Rosalind and the highborn characters in the play, as Sancho Panza provided homely humor to contrast with the high-flown notions of Don Quixote.

Although Shakespeare took over the absurd conventions of romance in plot and incident, he gave so much life and reality to his principal characters that his audience is willing to grant the illusions required of the plot. Readers of pastoral romances were accustomed to shepherds and shepherdesses wandering about rather aimlessly and penning sonnets to the objects of their affections. If these lovelorn folk encountered a dragon, a lion, or a unicorn, that was never surprising. If the villain met a saintly hermit and suddenly changed his way of life after a sermon from the holy man, that too was conventional and usual. It was never considered strange for maidens to go masquerading as pages or young warriors, and always disguises were so perfect that no father could tell his own daughter, nor a lover his own lady, though he might have spent the previous soliloquy mooning over the quality of her voice, the loveliness of her lips, or the color of her eyes. Such conventions Shakespeare took over part and parcel, but they do not trouble us any more than they troubled the author's contemporaries. We are concerned with other more compelling elements in *As You Like It*.

The modern reader or spectator still delights in the atmosphere of the play. He too smells the woods, the flowers, and the fresh fields of Arden or of whatever locality his imagination provides. It is a play for springtime and youth. Perhaps that is why it has been popular in schools and colleges for open-air performance.

The play is also filled with gaiety and humor of a quality that does not stale. Touchstone the fool is one of Shakespeare's most amusing comic characters and one that has given scope to many stage comedians. The first actor to play this part was Shakespeare's colleague Robert Armin, and Shakespeare obviously wrote the part for him. Armin had succeeded Will Kemp, the previous actor of clowning roles in Shakespeare's company, and some stage historians have seen a shift in the quality of the clowns with this change. The later fools or clowns are more intellectualized and wittier than the parts played by Kemp, who himself was famous for buffoonery and slapstick comedy.

Touchstone serves as a sort of chorus or a commentator on the action and the behavior of the other characters. When conversation becomes too lofty, especially when the sentiments of the lovers begin to soar away into metaphor, it is Touchstone who brings the tone down to earth with his homespun comments. When others talk of ethereal love, he exemplifies the physical desires felt by ordinary folk. He recognizes that "wedlock would be nibbling," and he remarks to Audrey: "Come, sweet Audrey./ We must be married, or we must live in bawdry."

Rosalind is typical of the heroines of pastoral romance only in external appearance, because her

Thomas Morley's musical setting of "It Was a Lover and His Lass."
From *The First Book of Ayres* (1600).

manner is too genuine and lifelike for the usual romance. Though she is madly in love with Orlando, she can play a practical joke upon him and make witty jests about lovers, a trait not characteristic of the weepy maidens in most of the prose tales. Not one of them, even masquerading as some other character, would have said, as Rosalind commented, that "Men have died from time to time, and worms have eaten them, but not for love." Rosalind is one of Shakespeare's most attractive women—witty, frank, generous, and courageous. The role has been a favorite with many of the most attractive actresses of the past century and a half.

Shakespeare exhibits assurance, ease, and originality in *As You Like It*. He was a successful playwright and he was conscious of his own ability to handle the theme with professional skill. But the play represents more than a new height of professional competence. It shows an adjustment to the world in which the author lived and a wholesome delight in the universe around him. Although critics have speculated on the significance of the melancholy Jaques and the possible reflection in his commentary of personal attitudes of the author, such speculation is beside the point. Jaques is of a type fashionable on the stage at that moment. Although he is not the typical malcontent whose cynicism was a popular theatrical convention in the last decade of the sixteenth century, he does represent a rather conventional type that affected a melancholy and dyspeptic attitude toward the world. As such he was amusing to the audiences of the time, but from the happy tone of the play there is no suggestion that Shakespeare meant Jaques to speak the author's own sentiments. Indeed, the spirit of the play is that of wholesome satisfaction with a world that is essentially good. Even the usurping Duke in the end undergoes a conversion and surrenders his lands to the rightful owner, and it is significant that Shakespeare is too charitable to have him killed in battle as Lodge had done in his novel.

In *As You Like It* Shakespeare studied the effects of love as it manifested itself in a variety of individuals: spirited and highborn Rosalind; brave and desperate Orlando; earthy Touchstone, content for a time with Audrey, "an ill-favored thing . . . but mine own"; selfish and thoughtless Phebe; faithful and loyal Silvius; and all the rest who are touched with an emotion universal in its influence upon men and women. Nowhere in the play does the treatment of this theme suggest anything but a healthy attitude. Shakespeare had looked on love and been content with what he found.

DATE, TEXT, AND STAGE HISTORY

The best evidence indicates that *As You Like It* was first performed between 1598 and 1600. It is not mentioned by Francis Meres in an enumeration of plays popular in 1598, but there is an entry in the *Stationers' Register* for August 4, 1600, of "As you like yt, a booke, to be staid." This would suggest a performance between these dates, probably close to the time that someone forbade its printing. The dating of about 1600 is as accurate as we can come to the first performance.

No quarto edition is known and the play originally saw print in the First Folio of 1623. This version presents a fairly good text with relatively few misprints. It is of course the basis of all modern editions. Since the Folio text contains few stage directions, modern editors have added enough to make the action understandable.

Where the play was first performed the text does not indicate. It was probably the Globe, which Shakespeare's company had opened in 1599. Their rivals, the Lord Admiral's Men, had attracted attention in 1598 with plays on the Robin Hood theme, and perhaps *As You Like It* was Shakespeare's effort to supply a competing play with a pastoral setting, which Henslowe's actors had found popular. The motion-picture companies in Hollywood are not the first dramatic groups to follow one another like sheep in trying to capture the public interest.

We can surmise that Shakespeare's play was a success, but direct evidence is lacking. A nineteenth-century historian, William Cory, claimed to know about a letter describing a performance of *As You Like It* at the Earl of Pembroke's house at Wilton in 1603 before King James I, but no one since has seen the letter and this may be a myth.

When the theatres reopened after the Restoration

Mrs. Siddons as Rosalind.
From an undated acting version of *As You Like It* used by the
Theatre Royal in Drury Lane, London.

of King Charles II, *As You Like It* was one of the plays allowed to be acted in 1669 at the Theatre Royal in Drury Lane. This comedy, however, was too fresh and clean for the jaded appetites of Restoration courtiers, and there is no record that it was popular until many years later.

In 1723, Charles Johnson produced at Drury Lane a hodgepodge from *As You Like It, Much Ado About Nothing,* and *A Midsummer Night's Dream* which he called *Love in a Forest,* but it was not until 1740 that Drury Lane got around to producing the play in its original form. This time it appeared with musical settings for the songs by Thomas Arne.

The spirit of romanticism was beginning to sweep the stage and *As You Like It* came into its own. Many of the most famous actresses played the part of Rosalind: Peg Woffington, Perdita Robinson, and Mrs. Sarah Siddons. During the nineteenth century, *As You Like It* was one of the most popular of Shakespeare's plays and it saw constant revivals. Among the famous Rosalinds of the nineteenth and twentieth centuries have been Charlotte Cushman, Helen Faucit, Ellen Tree, Ada Rehan, Mrs. Pat Campbell, Viola Allen, Julia Marlowe, and Edith Evans. The leading actors have taken the roles of Orlando and Jaques, and some of the best comedians have played Touchstone. *As You Like It* provides an opportunity for many good roles in addition to Rosalind, always the star part.

Operatic versions were popular in the early decades of the nineteenth century, and these musical versions often slighted the poetry of the original author while leaning heavily on the skill of the musicians and scene painters. The later nineteenth century purged away most of the extraneous trappings and presented the play as Shakespeare wrote it.

This comedy has remained a favorite on both the professional and amateur stages. College dramatic societies and "little theatre" groups find it an attractive medium for their efforts.

THE AUTHOR

As early as 1598 Shakespeare was so well known as a literary and dramatic craftsman that Francis Meres, in his *Palladis Tamia: Wits Treasury*, referred in flattering terms to him as "mellifluous and honey-tongued Shakespeare," famous for his *Venus and Adonis*, his *Lucrece*, and "his sugared sonnets," which were circulating "among his private friends." Meres observes further that "as Plautus and Seneca are accounted the best for comedy and tragedy among the Latins, so Shakespeare among the English is the most excellent in both kinds for the stage," and he mentions a dozen plays that had made a name for Shakespeare. He concludes with the remark "that the Muses would speak with Shakespeare's fine filed phrase if they would speak English."

To those acquainted with the history of the Elizabethan and Jacobean periods, it is incredible that anyone should be so naïve or ignorant as to doubt the reality of Shakespeare as the author of the plays that bear his name. Yet so much nonsense has been written about other "candidates" for the plays that it is well to remind readers that no credible evidence that would stand up in a court of law has ever been adduced to prove either that Shakespeare did not write his plays or that anyone else wrote them. All the theories offered for the authorship of Francis Bacon, the Earl of Derby, the Earl of Oxford, the Earl of Hertford, Christopher Marlowe, and a score of other candidates are mere conjectures spun from the active imaginations of persons who confuse hypothesis and conjecture with evidence.

As Meres' statement of 1598 indicates, Shakespeare was already a popular playwright whose name carried weight at the box office. The obvious reputation of Shakespeare as early as 1598 makes the effort to prove him a myth one of the most absurd in the history of human perversity.

The anti-Shakespeareans talk darkly about a plot of vested interests to maintain the authorship of Shakespeare. Nobody has any vested interest in Shakespeare, but every scholar is interested in the truth and in the quality of evidence advanced by special pleaders who set forth hypotheses in place of facts.

The anti-Shakespeareans base their arguments upon a few simple premises, all of them false. These false premises are that Shakespeare was an unlettered yokel without any schooling, that nothing is known about Shakespeare, and that only a noble lord or the equivalent in background could have written the plays. The facts are that more is known about Shakespeare than about most dramatists of his day, that he had a very good education, acquired in the Stratford Grammar School, that the plays show no evidence of profound book learning, and that the knowledge of kings and courts evident in the plays is no greater than any intelligent young man could have picked up at second hand. Most anti-Shakespeareans are naïve and betray an obvious snobbery. The author of their favorite plays, they imply, must have had a college diploma framed and hung on his study wall like the one in their dentist's office, and obviously so great a writer must have had a title or some equally significant evidence of exalted social background. They forget that genius has a way of cropping up in unexpected places and that none of the great creative writers of the world got his inspiration in a college or university course.

William Shakespeare was the son of John Shakespeare of Stratford-upon-Avon, a substantial citizen of that small but busy market town in the center of the rich agricultural county of Warwick. John Shakespeare kept a shop, what we would call a general store; he dealt in wool and other produce and gradually acquired property. As a youth, John Shakespeare had learned the trade of glover and leather worker. There is no contemporary evidence that the elder Shakespeare was a butcher, though the anti-Shakespeareans like to talk about the ignorant "butcher's boy of Stratford." Their only evidence is a statement by gossipy John Aubrey, more than a century after William Shakespeare's birth, that young William followed his father's trade, and when he killed a calf, "he would do it in a high style and make a speech." We would like to believe the story true, but Aubrey is not a very credible witness.

John Shakespeare probably continued to operate a farm at Snitterfield that his father had leased. He married Mary Arden, daughter of his father's landlord, a man of some property. The third of their eight children was William, baptized on April 26, 1564, and probably born three days before. At least, it is conventional to celebrate April 23 as his birthday.

The Stratford records give considerable information about John Shakespeare. We know that he held several municipal offices including those of alderman and mayor. In 1580 he was in some sort of legal difficulty and was fined for neglecting a summons of the Court of Queen's Bench requiring him to appear at Westminster and be bound over to keep the peace.

As a citizen and alderman of Stratford, John Shakespeare was entitled to send his son to the grammar school free. Though the records are lost, there can be no reason to doubt that this is where young William received his education. As any student of the period knows, the grammar schools provided the basic education in Latin learning and literature. The Elizabethan grammar school is not to be confused with modern grammar schools. Many cultivated men of the day received all their formal education in the grammar schools. At the universities in this period a student would have received little training that would have inspired him to be a creative writer. At Stratford young Shakespeare would have acquired a familiarity with Latin and some little knowledge of Greek. He would have read Latin authors and become acquainted with the plays of Plautus and Terence. Undoubtedly, in this period of his life he received that stimulation to read and explore for himself the world of ancient and modern history which he later utilized in his plays. The youngster who does not acquire this type of intellectual curiosity *before* college days rarely develops as a result of a college course the kind of mind Shakespeare demonstrated. His learning in books was anything but profound, but he clearly had the probing curiosity that sent him in search of information, and he had a keenness in the observation of nature and of humankind that finds reflection in his poetry.

There is little documentation for Shakespeare's boyhood. There is little reason why there should be. Nobody knew that he was going to be a dramatist about whom any scrap of information would be prized in the centuries to come. He was merely an active and vigorous youth of Stratford, perhaps assisting his father in his business, and no Boswell bothered to write down facts about him. The most important record that we have is a marriage license issued by the Bishop of Worcester on November 28, 1582, to permit William Shakespeare to marry Anne Hathaway, seven or eight years his senior; furthermore, the Bishop permitted the marriage after reading the banns only once instead of three times, evidence of the desire for haste. The need was explained on May 26, 1583, when the christening of Susanna, daughter of William and Anne Shakespeare, was recorded at Stratford. Two years later, on February 2, 1585, the records show the birth of twins to the Shakespeares, a boy and a girl who were christened Hamnet and Judith.

What William Shakespeare was doing in Stratford during the early years of his married life, or when he went to London, we do not know. It has been conjectured that he tried his hand at schoolteaching, but that is a mere guess. There is a legend that he left Stratford to escape a charge of poaching in the park of Sir Thomas Lucy of Charlecote, but there is no proof of this. There is also a legend that when first he came to London, he earned his living by holding horses outside a playhouse and presently was given employment inside, but there is nothing better than eighteenth-century hearsay for this. How Shakespeare broke into the London theatres as a dramatist and actor we do not know. But lack of information is not surprising, for Elizabethans did not write their autobiographies, and we know even less about the lives of many writers and some men of affairs than we know about Shakespeare. By 1592 he was so well established and popular that he incurred the envy of the dramatist and pamphleteer Robert Greene, who referred to him as an "upstart crow . . . in his own conceit the only Shake-scene in a country." From this time onward, contemporary allusions and references in legal documents enable the scholar to chart Shakespeare's career with greater accuracy than is possible with most other Elizabethan dramatists.

By 1594 Shakespeare was a member of the company of actors known as the Lord Chamberlain's Men. After the accession of James I, in 1603, the company would have the sovereign for their patron and would be known as the King's Men. During the period of its greatest prosperity, this company would have as its principal theatres the Globe and the Blackfriars. Shakespeare was both an actor and a shareholder in the company. Tradition has assigned him such acting roles as Adam in *As You Like It* and the Ghost in *Hamlet*, a modest place on the stage that suggests that he may have had other duties in the management of the company. Such conclusions, however, are based on surmise.

What we do know is that his plays were popular and that he was highly successful in his vocation. His first play may have been *The Comedy of Errors*, acted perhaps in 1591. Certainly this was one of his earliest plays. The three parts of *Henry VI* were acted sometime between 1590 and 1592. Critics are not in agreement about precisely how much Shakespeare wrote of these three plays. *Richard III* probably dates from 1593. With this play Shakespeare captured the imagination of Elizabethan audiences, then enormously interested in historical plays. With *Richard III* Shakespeare also gave an interpretation pleasing to the Tudors of the rise to power of the grandfather of Queen Elizabeth. From this time onward, Shakespeare's plays followed on the stage in rapid succession: *Titus Andronicus, The Taming of the Shrew, The Two Gentlemen of Verona, Love's Labour's Lost, Romeo and Juliet, Richard II, A Midsummer Night's Dream, King John, The Merchant of Venice, Henry IV*, Pts. I and II, *Much Ado About Nothing, Henry V, Julius Cæsar, As You Like It, Twelfth Night, Hamlet, The Merry Wives of Windsor, All's Well That Ends Well, Measure for Measure, Othello, King Lear*, and nine others that followed before Shakespeare retired completely, about 1613.

In the course of his career in London, he made enough money to enable him to retire to Stratford with a competence. His purchase on May 4, 1597, of New Place, then the second-largest dwelling in Stratford, a "pretty house of brick and timber," with a handsome garden, indicates his increasing prosperity. There his wife and children lived while he busied himself in the London theatres. The summer before he acquired New Place, his life was darkened by the death of his only son, Hamnet, a child of eleven. In May, 1602, Shakespeare purchased one hundred and seven acres of fertile farmland near Stratford and a few months later bought a cottage and garden across the alley from New Place. About 1611, he seems to have returned permanently to Stratford, for the next year a legal document refers to him as "William Shakespeare of Stratford-upon-Avon . . . gentleman." To achieve the desired appellation of gentleman, William Shakespeare had seen to it that the College of Heralds in 1596 granted his father a coat of arms. In one step he thus became a second-generation gentleman.

Shakespeare's daughter Susanna made a good match in 1607 with Dr. John Hall, a prominent and prosperous Stratford physician. His second daughter, Judith, did not marry until she was thirty-two years old, and then, under somewhat scandalous circumstances, she married Thomas Quiney, a Stratford vintner. On March 25, 1616, Shakespeare made his will, bequeathing his landed property to Susanna, £300 to Judith, certain sums to other relatives, and his second-best bed to his wife, Anne. Much has been made of the second-best bed, but the legacy probably indicates only that Anne liked that particular bed. Shakespeare, following the practice of the time, may have already arranged with Susanna for his wife's care. Finally, on April 23, 1616, the anniversary of his birth, William Shakespeare died, and he was buried on April 25 within the chancel of Trinity Church, as befitted an honored citizen. On August 6, 1623, a few months before the publication of the collected edition of Shakespeare's plays, Anne Shakespeare joined her husband in death.

THE PUBLICATION OF HIS PLAYS

During his lifetime Shakespeare made no effort to publish any of his plays, though eighteen appeared in print in single-play editions known as quartos. Some of these are corrupt versions known as "bad quartos." No quarto, so far as is known, had the author's approval. Plays were not considered "literature" any more than most radio and television scripts today are considered literature. Dramatists sold their plays outright to the theatrical companies and it was usually considered in the company's interest to keep plays from getting into print. To achieve a reputation as a man of letters, Shakespeare wrote his *Sonnets* and his narrative poems, *Venus and Adonis* and *The Rape of Lucrece*, but he probably never dreamed that his plays would establish his reputation as a literary genius. Only Ben Jonson, a man known for his colossal conceit, had the crust to call his plays *Works*, as he did when he published an edition in 1616. But men laughed at Ben Jonson.

After Shakespeare's death, two of his old colleagues in the King's Men, John Heminges and Henry Condell, decided that it would be a good thing to print, in more accurate versions than were then available, the plays already published and eighteen additional plays not previously published in quarto. In 1623 appeared *Mr. William Shakespeares Comedies, Histories, & Tragedies. Published according to the True Originall Copies. London. Printed by Isaac Iaggard and Ed. Blount.* This was the famous First Folio, a work that had the authority of Shakespeare's associates. The only play commonly attributed to Shakespeare that was omitted in the First Folio was *Pericles.* In their preface, "To the great Variety of Readers," Heminges and Condell state that whereas "you were abused with diverse stolen and surreptitious copies, maimed and deformed by the frauds and stealths of injurious impostors that exposed them, even those are now offered to your view cured and perfect of their limbs; and all the rest, absolute in their numbers, as he conceived them." What they used for printer's copy is one of the vexed problems of scholarship, and skilled bibliographers have devoted years of study to the question of the relation of the "copy" for the First Folio to Shakespeare's manuscripts. In some cases it is clear that the editors corrected printed quarto versions of the plays, probably by comparison with playhouse scripts. Whether these scripts were in Shakespeare's autograph is anybody's guess. No manuscript of any play in Shakespeare's handwriting has survived. Indeed, very few play manuscripts from this period by any author are extant. The Tudor and Stuart periods had not yet learned to prize autographs and authors' original manuscripts.

Since the First Folio contains eighteen plays not previously printed, it is the only source for these. For the other eighteen, which had appeared in quarto versions, the First Folio also has the authority of an edition prepared and overseen by Shakespeare's colleagues and professional associates. But since editorial standards in 1623 were far from strict, and Heminges and Condell were actors rather than editors by profession, the texts are sometimes careless. The printing and proofreading of the First Folio also left much to be desired, and some garbled passages have to be corrected and emended. The "good quarto" texts have to be taken into account in preparing a modern edition.

Because of the great popularity of Shakespeare through the centuries, the First Folio has become a prized book, but it is not a very rare one, for it is estimated that 238 copies are extant. The Folger Shakespeare Library in Washington, D.C., has seventy-nine copies of the First Folio, collected by the founder, Henry Clay Folger, who believed that a collection of as many texts as possible would reveal significant facts about the text of Shakespeare's plays. Dr. Charlton Hinman, using an ingenious machine of his own invention for mechanical collating, has made many discoveries that throw light on Shakespeare's text and on printing practices of the day.

The probability is that the First Folio of 1623 had an edition of between 1,000 and 1,250 copies. It is believed that it sold for £1, which made it an expensive book, for £1 in 1623 was equivalent to something between $40 and $50 in modern purchasing power.

During the seventeenth century, Shakespeare was sufficiently popular to warrant three later editions in folio size, the Second Folio of 1632, the Third Folio of 1663–1664, and the Fourth Folio of 1685. The Third Folio added six other plays ascribed to Shakespeare, but these are apocryphal.

THE SHAKESPEAREAN THEATRE

The theatres in which Shakespeare's plays were performed were vastly different from those we know today. The stage was a platform that jutted out into the area now occupied by the first rows of seats on the main floor, what is called the "orchestra" in America and the "pit" in England. This platform had no curtain to come down at the ends of acts and scenes. And although simple stage properties were available, the Elizabethan theatre lacked both the machinery and the elaborate movable scenery of the modern theatre. In the rear of the platform stage was a curtained area that could be used as an inner room, a tomb, or any such scene that might be required. A balcony above this inner room, and perhaps balconies on the sides of the stage, could represent the upper deck of a ship, the entry to Juliet's room, or a prison window. A trap door in the stage provided an entrance for ghosts and devils from the nether regions, and a similar trap in the canopied structure over the stage, known as the "heavens," made it possible to let down angels on a rope. These primitive stage arrangements help to account for many elements in Elizabethan plays. For example, since there was no curtain, the dramatist frequently felt the necessity of writing into his play action to clear the stage at the ends of acts and scenes. The funeral march at the end of *Hamlet* is not there merely for atmosphere; Shakespeare had to get the corpses off the stage. The lack of scenery also freed the dramatist from undue concern about the exact location of his sets, and the physical relation of his various settings to each other did not have to be worked out with the same precision as in the modern theatre.

Before London had buildings designed exclusively for theatrical entertainment, plays were given in inns and taverns. The characteristic inn of the period had an inner courtyard with rooms opening onto balconies overlooking the yard. Players could set up their temporary stages at one end of the yard and audiences could find seats on the balconies out of the weather. The poorer sort could stand or sit on the cobblestones in the yard, which was open to the sky. The first theatres followed this construction, and throughout the Elizabethan period the large public theatres had a yard in front of the stage open to the weather, with two or three

tiers of covered balconies extending around the
theatre. This physical structure again influenced
the writing of plays. Because a dramatist wanted
the actors to be heard, he frequently wrote into his
play orations that could be delivered with declama-
tory effect. He also provided spectacle, buffoonery,
and broad jests to keep the riotous groundlings in
the yard entertained and quiet.

In another respect the Elizabethan theatre dif-
fered greatly from ours. It had no actresses. All
women's roles were taken by boys, sometimes re-
cruited from the boy's choirs of the London
churches. Some of thees youths acted their roles
with great skill and the Elizabethans did not seem
to be aware of any incongruity. The first actresses
on the professional English stage appeared after
the Restoration of Charles II, in 1660, when exiled
Englishmen brought back from France practices of
the French stage.

London in the Elizabethan period, as now, was
the center of theatrical interest, though wandering
actors from time to time traveled through the country performing in inns, halls, and the houses of the
nobility. The first professional playhouse, called
simply The Theatre, was erected by James Burbage,
father of Shakespeare's colleague Richard Burbage,
in 1576 on lands of the old Holywell Priory adjacent
to Finsbury Fields, a playground and park area
just north of the city walls. It had the advantage of
being outside the city's jurisdiction and yet was

near enough to be easily accessible. Soon after The Theatre was opened, another playhouse called The Curtain was erected in the same neighborhood. Both of these playhouses had open courtyards and were probably polygonal in shape.

About the time The Curtain opened, Richard Farrant, Master of the Children of the Chapel Royal at Windsor and of St. Paul's, conceived the idea of opening a "private" theatre in the old monastery buildings of the Blackfriars, not far from St. Paul's Cathedral in the heart of the city. This theatre was ostensibly to train the choirboys in plays for presentation at Court, but Farrant managed to present plays to paying audiences and achieved considerable success until aristocratic neighbors complained and had the theatre closed. This first Blackfriars Theatre was significant, however, because it popularized the boy actors in a professional way and it paved the way for a second theatre in the Blackfriars, which Shakespeare's company took over more than thirty years later. By the last years of the sixteenth century, London had at least six professional theatres and still others were erected during the reign of James I.

The Globe Theatre, the playhouse that most people connect with Shakespeare, was erected early in 1599 on the Bankside, the area across the Thames from the city. Its construction had a dramatic beginning, for on the night of December 28, 1598, James Burbage's sons, Cuthbert and Richard, gathered together a crew who tore down the old theatre

The Globe Playhouse.
From Visscher's *View of London* (1616).

in Holywell and carted the timbers across the river to a site that they had chosen for a new playhouse. The reason for this clandestine operation was a row with the landowner over the lease to the Holywell property. The site chosen for the Globe was another playground outside of the city's jurisdiction, a region of somewhat unsavory character. Not far away was the Bear Garden, an amphitheatre devoted to the baiting of bears and bulls. This was also the region occupied by many houses of ill fame licensed by the Bishop of Winchester and the source of substantial revenue to him. But it was easily accessible either from London Bridge or by means of the cheap boats operated by the London watermen, and it had the great advantage of being beyond the authority of the Puritanical aldermen of London, who frowned on plays because they lured apprentices from work, filled their heads with improper ideas, and generally exerted a bad influence. The aldermen also complained that the crowds drawn together in the theatre helped to spread the plague.

The Globe was the handsomest theatre up to its time. It was a large building, apparently octagonal in shape and open like its predecessors to the sky in the center, but capable of seating a large audience in its covered balconies. To erect and operate the Globe, the Burbages organized a syndicate composed of the leading members of the dramatic company, of which Shakespeare was a member.

tectum

ades

planities sive arena

Interior of the Swan Theatre.
From a drawing by Johannes de Witt (1596).

Since it was open to the weather and depended on natural light, plays had to be given in the afternoon. This caused no hardship in the long afternoons of an English summer, but in the winter the weather was a great handicap and discouraged all except the hardiest. For that reason, in 1608 Shakespeare's company was glad to take over the lease of the second Blackfriars Theatre, a substantial, roomy hall reconstructed within the framework of the old monastery building. This theatre was protected from the weather and its stage was artificially lighted by chandeliers of candles. This became the winter playhouse for Shakespeare's company and at once proved so popular that the congestion of traffic created an embarrassing problem. Stringent regulations had to be made for the movement of coaches in the vicinity. Shakespeare's company continued to use the Globe during the summer months. In 1613 a squib fired from a cannon during a performance of *Henry VIII* fell on the thatched roof and the Globe burned to the ground. The next year it was rebuilt.

London had other famous theatres. The Rose, just west of the Globe, was built by Philip Henslowe, a semiliterate denizen of the Bankside, who became one of the most important theatrical owners and producers of the Tudor and Stuart periods. What is more important for historians, he kept a detailed account book, which provides much of our information about theatrical history in his time.

Another famous theatre on the Bankside was the Swan, which a Dutch priest, Johannes de Witt, visited in 1596. The crude drawing of the stage which he made was copied by his friend Arend van Buchell; it is one of the important pieces of contemporary evidence for theatrical construction. Among the other theatres, the Fortune, north of the city, on Golding Lane, and the Red Bull, even farther away from the city, off St. John's Street, were the most popular. The Red Bull, much frequented by apprentices, favored sensational and sometimes rowdy plays.

The actors who kept all of these theatres going were organized into companies under the protection of some noble patron. Traditionally actors had enjoyed a low reputation. In some of the ordinances they were classed as vagrants; in the phraseology of the time, "rogues, vagabonds, sturdy beggars, and common players" were all listed together as undesirables. To escape penalties often meted out to these characters, organized groups of actors managed to gain the protection of various personages of high degree. In the later years of Elizabeth's reign, a group flourished under the name of the Queen's Men; another group had the protection of the Lord Admiral and were known as the Lord Admiral's Men. Edward Alleyn, son-in-law of Philip Henslowe, was the leading spirit in the Lord Admiral's Men. Besides the adult companies, troupes of boy actors from time to time also enjoyed considerable popularity. Among these were the Children of Paul's and the Children of the Chapel Royal.

The company with which Shakespeare had a long association had for its first patron Henry Carey, Lord Hunsdon, the Lord Chamberlain, and hence they were known as the Lord Chamberlain's Men. After the accession of James I, they became the King's Men. This company was the great rival of the Lord Admiral's Men, managed by Henslowe and Alleyn.

All was not easy for the players in Shakespeare's time, for the aldermen of London were always eager for an excuse to close up the Blackfriars and any other theatres in their jurisdiction. The theatres outside the jurisdiction of London were not immune from interference, for they might be shut up by order of the Privy Council for meddling in politics or for various other offenses, or they might be closed in time of plague lest they spread infection. During plague times, the actors usually went on tour and played the provinces wherever they could find an audience. Particularly frightening were the plagues of 1592–1594 and 1613 when the theatres closed and the players, like many other Londoners, had to take to the country.

Though players had a low social status, they enjoyed great popularity, and one of the favorite forms of entertainment at Court was the performance of plays. To be commanded to perform at Court conferred great prestige upon a company of players, and printers frequently noted that fact when they published plays. Several of Shakespeare's plays were performed before the sovereign, and Shakespeare himself undoubtedly acted in some of these plays.

REFERENCES FOR FURTHER READING

Many readers will want suggestions for further reading about Shakespeare and his times. The literature in this field is enormous but a few references will serve as guides to further study. A simple and useful little book is Gerald Sanders, *A Shakespeare Primer* (New York, 1950). *A Companion to Shakespeare Studies,* edited by Harley Granville-Barker and G. B. Harrison (Cambridge, Eng., 1934) is a valuable guide. More detailed but still not too voluminous to be confusing is Hazelton Spencer, *The Art and Life of William Shakespeare* (New York, 1940) which, like Sanders' handbook, contains a brief annotated list of useful books on various aspects of the subject. The most detailed and scholarly work providing complete factual information about Shakespeare is Sir Edmund Chambers, *William Shakespeare: A Study of Facts and Problems* (2 vols., Oxford, 1930). For detailed, factual information about the Elizabethan and seventeenth-century stages, the definitive reference works are Sir

Edmund Chambers, *The Elizabethan Stage* (4 vols., Oxford, 1923) and Gerald E. Bentley, *The Jacobean and Caroline Stage* (5 vols., Oxford, 1941–1956). Alfred Harbage, *Shakespeare's Audience* (New York, 1941) throws light on the nature and tastes of the customers for whom Elizabethan dramatists wrote.

Although specialists disagree about details of stage construction, the reader will find essential information in John C. Adams, *The Globe Playhouse: Its Design and Equipment* (Barnes & Noble, 1961). A model of the Globe playhouse by Dr. Adams is on permanent exhibition in the Folger Shakespeare Library in Washington, D.C. An excellent description of the architecture of the Globe is Irwin Smith, *Shakespeare's Globe Playhouse: A Modern Reconstruction in Text and Scale Drawings Based upon the Reconstruction of the Globe by John Cranford Adams* (New York, 1956). Another recent study of the physical characteristics of the Globe is C. Walter Hodges, *The Globe Restored* (London, 1953). An easily read history of the early theatres is J. Q. Adams, *Shakespearean Playhouses: A History of English Theatres from the Beginnings to the Restoration* (Boston, 1917).

The following titles on theatrical history will provide information about Shakespeare's plays in later periods: Alfred Harbage, *Theatre for Shakespeare* (Toronto, 1955); Esther Cloudman Dunn, *Shake-*

speare in America (New York, 1939); George C. D. Odell, *Shakespeare from Betterton to Irving* (2 vols., London, 1931); Arthur Colby Sprague, *Shakespeare and the Actors: The Stage Business in His Plays (1660–1905)* (Cambridge, Mass., 1944) and *Shakespearian Players and Performances* (Cambridge, Mass., 1953); Leslie Hotson, *The Commonwealth and Restoration Stage* (Cambridge, Mass., 1928); Alwin Thaler, *Shakspere to Sheridan: A Book About the Theatre of Yesterday and To-day* (Cambridge, Mass., 1922); Ernest Bradlee Watson, *Sheridan to Robertson: A Study of the 19th-Century London Stage* (Cambridge, Mass., 1926). Enid Welsford, *The Court Masque* (Cambridge, Mass., 1927) is an excellent study of the characteristics of this form of entertainment.

Harley Granville-Barker, *Prefaces to Shakespeare* (5 vols., London, 1927–1948) provides stimulating critical discussion of the plays. An older classic of criticism is Andrew C. Bradley, *Shakespearean Tragedy: Lectures on Hamlet, Othello, King Lear, Macbeth* (London, 1904), which is now available in an inexpensive reprint (New York, 1955). Thomas M. Parrot, *Shakespearean Comedy* (New York, 1949) is scholarly and readable. Shakespeare's dramatizations of English history are examined in E. M. W. Tillyard, *Shakespeare's History Plays* (London, 1948), and Lily Bess Campbell, *Shakespeare's "Histories," Mirrors of Elizabethan Policy* (San Marino,

Calif., 1947) contains a more technical discussion of the same subject.

The question of the authenticity of Shakespeare's plays arouses perennial attention. A book that demolishes the notion of hidden cryptograms in the plays is William F. Friedman and Elizebeth S. Friedman, *The Shakespearean Ciphers Examined* (New York, 1957). A succinct account of the various absurdities advanced to suggest the authorship of a multitude of candidates other than Shakespeare will be found in R. C. Churchill, *Shakespeare and His Betters* (Bloomington, Ind., 1959) and Frank W. Wadsworth, *The Poacher from Stratford: A Partial Account of the Controversy over the Authorship of Shakespeare's Plays* (Berkeley, Calif., 1958). An essay on the curious notions in the writings of the anti-Shakespeareans is that by Louis B. Wright, "The Anti-Shakespeare Industry and the Growth of Cults," *The Virginia Quarterly Review*, XXXV (1959), 289-303.

Reprints of some of the sources for Shakespeare's plays, including *As You Like It*, can be found in *Shakespeare's Library* (2 vols., 1850), edited by John Payne Collier, and *The Shakespeare Classics* (12 vols., 1907–1926), edited by Israel Gollancz. Thomas Lodge's *Rosalynde* has also been reprinted separately. Geoffrey Bullough, *Narrative and Dramatic Sources of Shakespeare* (New York, 1957) is a new series of volumes reprinting the sources. Two volumes covering the early comedies, comedies (1597–1603), and histories are now available. For discussion of Shakespeare's use of his sources see Kenneth Muir, *Shakespeare's Sources: Comedies and Tragedies* (London, 1957). Thomas M. Cranfill has recently edited a facsimile reprint of *Riche His Farewell to Military Profession* (1581), which contains stories that Shakespeare probably used for several of his plays.

A stimulating discussion of *As You Like It* in relation to some of the social customs of the times will be found in C. L. Barber, *Shakespeare's Festive Comedy: A Study of Dramatic Form and Its Relation to Social Custom* (Princeton, 1959).

Interesting pictures as well as new information about Shakespeare will be found in F. E. Halliday, *Shakespeare, a Pictorial Biography* (London, 1956). Allardyce Nicoll, *The Elizabethans* (Cambridge, Eng., 1957) contains a variety of illustrations.

A brief, clear, and accurate account of Tudor history is S. T. Bindoff, *The Tudors*, in the Penguin series. A readable general history is G. M. Trevelyan, *The History of England*, first published in 1926 and available in many editions. G. M. Trevelyan, *English Social History*, first published in 1942 and also available in many editions, provides fascinating information about England in all periods. Sir John Neale, *Queen Elizabeth* (London, 1934) is the best study of the great Queen. Various aspects of life in the Elizabethan period are treated in Louis B. Wright, *Middle-Class Culture in Elizabethan England* (Chapel Hill, N.C., 1935; reprinted by Cornell University Press, 1958). *Shakespeare's England: An Account of the Life and Manners of His Age,* edited by Sidney Lee and C. T. Onions (2 vols., Oxford, 1916), provides a large amount of information on many aspects of life in the Elizabethan period. Additional information will be found in Muriel St. C. Byrne, *Elizabethan Life in Town and Country* (Barnes & Noble, 1961).

The Folger Shakespeare Library is currently publishing a series of illustrated pamphlets on various aspects of English life in the sixteenth and seventeenth century. The following titles are available: Dorothy E. Mason, *Music in Elizabethan England;* Craig R. Thompson, *The English Church in the Sixteenth Century;* Louis B. Wright, *Shakespeare's Theatre and the Dramatic Tradition;* Giles E. Dawson, *The Life of William Shakespeare;* Virginia A. LaMar, *English Dress in the Age of Shakespeare;* Craig R. Thompson, *The Bible in English, 1525–1611;* Craig R. Thompson, *Schools in Tudor England;* Craig R. Thompson, *Universities in Tudor England;* Lilly C. Stone, *English Sports and Recreations;* Conyers Read, *The Government of England under Elizabeth;* Virginia A. LaMar, *Travel and Roads in England.*

[Dramatis Personae.

Duke Senior, exiled.
Duke Frederick, his brother and usurper of his
   dukedom.
Amiens, } lords attending on *Duke Senior*.
Jaques,
Le Beau, a courtier attending on *Duke Fred-
   erick*.
Charles, wrestler to *Duke Frederick*.
Oliver,
Jaques de Boys, } sons of *Sir Rowland de Boys*.
Orlando,
Adam, } servants to *Oliver*.
Dennis,
Touchstone, a clown.
Sir Oliver Martext, a vicar.
Corin, } shepherds.
Silvius,
William, a countryman, in love with *Audrey*.
Hymen, god of marriage.

Rosalind, daughter to *Duke Senior*.
Celia, daughter to *Duke Frederick*.
Phebe, a shepherdess.

Audrey, a country wench.

Lords, Pages, Attendants, &c.

Scene:—*Oliver's orchard; Duke Frederick's
      court; the Forest of Arden.*]

AS YOU LIKE IT

ACT I

I. i. Oliver, oldest son of Sir Rowland de Boys, has inherited his father's estate and kept the inheritance of a thousand crowns left to his younger brother Orlando. Orlando has been allowed nothing but bare subsistence and Oliver has even denied him schooling and training in the skills of a gentleman. Orlando's rebellion at this treatment merely hardens his brother against him. When Charles, the Duke's champion wrestler, reports that Orlando may challenge him, Oliver incites him to do his utmost by painting a black picture of his brother's evil nature. Though he privately recognizes Orlando's virtues, he hates him the more for them and will not be happy until he is rid of him.

\|\|\|\|\|\|\|\|\|\|\|\|\|\|\|\|\|\|\|\|\|\|\|\|\|\|\|\|\|\|\|\|\|\|\|\|\|\|\|\|\|\|\|\|\|\|\|\|

2. **poor a:** that is, a paltry thousand crowns.

4. **breed me:** train me up.

5. **keeps:** i.e., pays his way.

5-6. **report speaks goldenly of his profit:** he is said to be making excellent progress.

7. **stays:** holds. While Jaques is maintained at school, Orlando is merely kept (detained) at home.

11. **fair with their feeding;** well fed.

11-2. **taught their manage:** i.e., broken in and trained.

16. **something that nature gave me:** good breeding.

16-7. **his countenance seems to take from me:** i.e., his treatment of me seems to deny.

18. **hinds:** farm boys.

19-20. **mines my gentility with my education:** destroys my fundamental gentility by denying me a proper education. **Mines** means "undermines."

1

ACT I

Scene I. [Oliver's orchard.]

Enter *Orlando* and *Adam.*

Orl. As I remember, Adam, it was upon this fashion
bequeathed me by will but poor a thousand crowns,
and, as thou sayst, charged my brother on his blessing
to breed me well; and there begins my sadness. My
brother Jaques he keeps at school, and report speaks   5
goldenly of his profit. For my part, he keeps me rus-
tically at home or, to speak more properly, stays me
here at home unkept; for call you that keeping for a
gentleman of my birth that differs not from the stall-
ing of an ox? His horses are bred better; for, besides   10
that they are fair with their feeding, they are taught
their manage, and to that end riders dearly hired; but
I, his brother, gain nothing under him but growth, for
the which his animals on his dunghills are as much
bound to him as I. Besides this nothing that he so plen-   15
tifully gives me, the something that nature gave me his
countenance seems to take from me. He lets me feed
with his hinds, bars me the place of a brother, and, as
much as in him lies, mines my gentility with my education. This is it, Adam, that grieves me; and the spirit   20

I

26. **shake me up:** abuse me.

30. **Marry:** "by the Virgin Mary"; indeed.

33-4. **be naught awhile:** a North Country curse meaning "A mischief on you."

35-6. **Shall . . . spent:** Orlando implies that without ever having had his inheritance from his father, he is reduced to the beggary which the Prodigal Son knew when he had squandered his patrimony.

42-3. **in the gentle condition of blood you should so know me:** that is, as far as breeding is concerned you should see that I am your equal—of the same blood.

44. **courtesy of nations:** civilized usage—a matter of convention rather than a fact of nature.

An English formal garden.
From Johann Amos Comenius, *Orbis sensualium pictus* (1685).

of my father, which I think is within me, begins to
mutiny against this servitude. I will no longer endure
it, though yet I know no wise remedy how to avoid it.

Enter *Oliver.*

Adam. Yonder comes my master, your brother.

Orl. Go apart, Adam, and thou shalt hear how he 25
will shake me up.

[*Adam withdraws.*]

Oli. Now, sir, what make you here?

Orl. Nothing. I am not taught to make anything.

Oli. What mar you then, sir?

Orl. Marry, sir, I am helping you to mar that which 30
God made, a poor unworthy brother of yours, with
idleness.

Oli. Marry, sir, be better employed, and be naught
awhile!

Orl. Shall I keep your hogs and eat husks with 35
them? What prodigal portion have I spent that I
should come to such penury?

Oli. Know you where you are, sir?

Orl. O, sir, very well: here in your orchard.

Oli. Know you before whom, sir? 40

Orl. Ay, better than him I am before knows me. I
know you are my eldest brother, and in the gentle
condition of blood you should so know me. The
courtesy of nations allows you my better in that you
are the first born; but the same tradition takes not 45
away my blood, were there twenty brothers betwixt
us. I have as much of my father in me as you, albeit

48-9. **nearer to his reverence:** i.e., nearer to him in age and therefore in the right to respect.

51. **too young:** too like a headstrong and untrained child.

53. **villain:** a person of low birth. Oliver uses the term in the modern sense of "rascal," but Orlando is still obsessed with the question of breeding and takes the word at its earlier meaning.

59. **Thou hast railed on thyself:** i.e., you attack yourself when you attack my birth.

65-6. **obscuring and hiding from me all gentlemanlike qualities:** keeping me ignorant of proper instruction in the accomplishments of a gentleman.

69-70. **allottery:** allotment.

I confess your coming before me is nearer to his reverence.

Oli. What, boy!   [*Strikes at him.*]   50

Orl. Come, come, elder brother, you are too young in this.

Oli. Wilt thou lay hands on me, villain?

Orl. I am no villain. I am the youngest son of Sir Rowland de Boys; he was my father, and he is thrice   55
a villain that says such a father begot villains. Wert thou not my brother, I would not take this hand from thy throat till this other had pulled out thy tongue for saying so. Thou hast railed on thyself.

Adam. [*Returning*] Sweet masters, be patient! For   60
your father's remembrance, be at accord!

Oli. Let me go, I say.

Orl. I will not till I please. You shall hear me. My father charged you in his will to give me good education. You have trained me like a peasant, obscuring   65
and hiding from me all gentlemanlike qualities. The spirit of my father grows strong in me, and I will no longer endure it. Therefore allow me such exercises as may become a gentleman, or give me the poor allottery my father left me by testament. With that I   70
will go buy my fortunes.

Oli. And what wilt thou do? beg when that is spent? Well, sir, get you in. I will not long be troubled with you. You shall have some part of your will. I pray you leave me.   75

Orl. I will no further offend you than becomes me for my good.

Oli. Get you with him, you old dog!

82. **grow upon me:** outgrow the little space I would have you occupy and overflow into the space I have reserved for myself. Though the image is from horticulture, Oliver refers to Orlando's demands for more of his birthright.

83. **physic your rankness:** remedy your luxuriant growth; cut you down to size.

Adam. Is "old dog" my reward? Most true, I have
lost my teeth in your service. God be with my old   80
master! he would not have spoke such a word.

> *Exeunt Orlando, Adam.*

Oli. Is it even so? Begin you to grow upon me? I
will physic your rankness and yet give no thousand
crowns neither. Holla, Dennis!

Enter *Dennis.*

Den. Calls your worship?   85
Oli. Was not Charles, the Duke's wrestler, here to
speak with me?
Den. So please you, he is here at the door and im-
portunes access to you.
Oli. Call him in. [*Exit Dennis.*] 'Twill be a good   90
way; and tomorrow the wrestling is.

Enter *Charles.*

Cha. Good morrow to your worship.
Oli. Good Monsieur Charles! What's the new news
at the new court?
Cha. There's no news at the court, sir, but the old   95
news. That is, the old Duke is banished by his younger
brother the new Duke, and three or four loving lords
have put themselves into voluntary exile with him,
whose lands and revenues enrich the new Duke;
therefore he gives them good leave to wander.   100
Oli. Can you tell if Rosalind, the Duke's daughter,
be banished with her father?

110. **the Forest of Arden:** Shakespeare is thinking of Arden in Warwickshire, though the scene is actually set in the Ardennes forest in French Flanders.

113-14. **fleet the time:** make the time pass swiftly by; **the golden world:** the Golden Age of classical mythology, when mankind was free of sin and had no need to work.

117. **Marry do I:** I do indeed.

120. **a fall:** i.e., one bout.

122-23. **acquit him well:** make a good showing for himself.

123-24. **for your love:** because of our friendship; **foil:** defeat.

128. **brook . . . well:** take with a good grace.

132. **requite:** reward.

Cha. O, no! for the Duke's daughter her cousin so loves her, being ever from their cradles bred together, that she would have followed her exile, or have died 105 to stay behind her. She is at the court, and no less beloved of her uncle than his own daughter, and never two ladies loved as they do.

Oli. Where will the old Duke live?

Cha. They say he is already in the Forest of Arden, 110 and a many merry men with him; and there they live like the old Robin Hood of England. They say many young gentlemen flock to him every day, and fleet the time carelessly as they did in the golden world.

Oli. What, you wrestle tomorrow before the new 115 Duke?

Cha. Marry do I, sir; and I came to acquaint you with a matter. I am given, sir, secretly to understand that your younger brother, Orlando, hath a disposition to come in disguised against me to try a fall. To- 120 morrow, sir, I wrestle for my credit, and he that escapes me without some broken limb shall acquit him well. Your brother is but young and tender, and for your love I would be loath to foil him, as I must for my own honor if he come in. Therefore, out of my 125 love to you, I came hither to acquaint you withal, that either you might stay him from his intendment, or brook such disgrace well as he shall run into, in that it is a thing of his own search and altogether against my will. 130

Oli. Charles, I thank thee for thy love to me, which thou shalt find I will most kindly requite. I had my-

134. by underhand means: indirectly; without attempting straightforward argument lest it strengthen his determination.

135-36. stubbornest: most obstinate and inclined to violence to gain his way. Shakespeare often uses the word "stubborn" in an earlier sense which implied fierce opposition rather than mere immovable determination.

137. envious emulator: envious often means "malicious." Combined with **emulator,** it adds to Oliver's characterization of his brother as a person so perverse and ill-natured that he cannot bear to see anyone else successful.

138. natural: i.e., by birth.

139. I had as lief: I would be just as pleased if.

140-41. thou wert best: you had better.

142. grace: honor.

143. practice: plot.

145. indirect: underhand; dishonest.

147-48. I speak but brotherly of him: that is, because he is my brother I speak more gently of his faults than he deserves; **anatomize:** dissect; take apart and analyze thoroughly.

153. go alone: i.e., walk upright without aid. Charles intends to use his strength and skill to insure that Orlando will be crippled if he is not killed.

156. stir this gamester: stir up Orlando's sporting instinct so that he will compete in the wrestling.

158. gentle: completely gentlemanly.

159. noble device: noble impulse; i.e., he is noble spirited.

159-60. enchantingly beloved: adored as if he had enchanted the beholders.

162. misprized: scorned.

self notice of my brother's purpose herein and have
by underhand means labored to dissuade him from it;
but he is resolute. I'll tell thee, Charles, it is the stub- 135
bornest young fellow of France; full of ambition, an
envious emulator of every man's good parts, a secret
and villainous contriver against me his natural
brother. Therefore use thy discretion. I had as lief
thou didst break his neck as his finger. And thou wert 140
best look to't; for if thou dost him any slight disgrace,
or if he do not mightily grace himself on thee, he will
practice against thee by poison, entrap thee by some
treacherous device, and never leave thee till he hath
ta'en thy life by some indirect means or other; for I 145
assure thee (and almost with tears I speak it) there is
not one so young and so villainous this day living. I
speak but brotherly of him; but should I anatomize
him to thee as he is, I must blush and weep, and thou
must look pale and wonder. 150

Cha. I am heartily glad I came hither to you. If he
come tomorrow, I'll give him his payment. If ever he
go alone again, I'll never wrestle for prize more. And
so God keep your worship!

Oli. Farewell, good Charles. *Exit [Charles].* Now 155
will I stir this gamester. I hope I shall see an end of
him, for my soul (yet I know not why) hates nothing
more than he. Yet he's gentle; never schooled and yet
learned; full of noble device; of all sorts enchantingly
beloved, and indeed so much in the heart of the 160
world, and especially of my own people, who best
know him, that I am altogether misprized. But it shall

164. kindle . . . thither: i.e., fire with enthusiasm for the wrestling.

I. ii. Celia and Rosalind, devoted cousins, make their first appearance. Celia is the daughter of the present Duke, who has banished his older brother, the father of Rosalind, and usurped his dukedom. Celia consoles Rosalind, who misses her father, and they are exchanging merry quips when it is reported that the wrestlers will complete their competition near by.

Charles has defeated and injured three challengers and it is Orlando's turn for a bout. Celia and Rosalind try to dissuade him from his purpose, but he is determined and, to everyone's surprise, he throws Charles. The Duke compliments Orlando, but when he discovers that Orlando's father was Rowland de Boys, an old enemy, he leaves abruptly. Rosalind has fallen in love with Orlando and parts from him reluctantly. Orlando, also in love with Rosalind, is at a loss for words when Rosalind attempts further conversation.

---

1. **merry:** cheerful (not "gay").

2-3. **I show more mirth than I am mistress of:** in other words, the cheer she is displaying is assumed.

5. **learn:** teach, as in modern ungrammatical speech.

10. **so:** if; provided that.

12-3. **righteously tempered:** tempered of the right ingredients.

19. **perforce:** forcibly; **render . . . again:** repay.

not be so long; this wrestler shall clear all. Nothing
remains but that I kindle the boy thither, which now
I'll go about.   165

Exit.

Scene II. [A lawn before the Duke's Palace.]

Enter *Rosalind* and *Celia.*

Cel. I pray thee, Rosalind, sweet my coz, be merry.

Ros. Dear Celia, I show more mirth than I am
mistress of, and would you yet I were merrier? Unless
you could teach me to forget a banished father, you
must not learn me how to remember any extraordinary   5
pleasure.

Cel. Herein I see thou lovest me not with the full
weight that I love thee. If my uncle, thy banished
father, had banished thy uncle, the Duke my father,
so thou hadst been still with me, I could have taught 10
my love to take thy father for mine. So wouldst thou,
if the truth of thy love to me were so righteously
tempered as mine is to thee.

Ros. Well, I will forget the condition of my estate
to rejoice in yours.   15

Cel. You know my father hath no child but I, nor
none is like to have; and truly, when he dies, thou
shalt be his heir; for what he hath taken away from
thy father perforce, I will render thee again in affection. By mine honor, I will! and when I break that   20

26. **in good earnest:** in reality, instead of in jest.

27. **with safety of a pure blush:** unmarked by shame, blushing only because of virgin modesty.

30-1. **the good housewife Fortune from her wheel: Fortune** was often described and pictured as controlling human destiny by the turn of her wheel. In general the wheel signified the inconstancy and unpredictability of **Fortune.** Here, however, Celia identifies it with a spinning wheel. **Housewife** frequently meant "hussy," "wanton"; Celia puns on this and the obvious meaning of the word.

37. **honest:** chaste.

45. **argument:** discussion—the tenor of the conversation, not a disagreement.

47. **Nature's natural:** that is, an idiot. Though Touchstone does not appear to be mentally deficient, many professional jesters were.

Fortune's wheel.
From Gregor Reisch, *Margarita philosophica* (1517).

oath, let me turn monster. Therefore, my sweet Rose,
my dear Rose, be merry.

Ros. From henceforth I will, coz, and devise sports.
Let me see. What think you of falling in love?

Cel. Marry, I prithee do, to make sport withal! But   25
love no man in good earnest, nor no further in sport
neither than with safety of a pure blush thou mayst in
honor come off again.

Ros. What shall be our sport then?

Cel. Let us sit and mock the good housewife For-   30
tune from her wheel, that her gifts may henceforth
be bestowed equally.

Ros. I would we could do so, for her benefits are
mightily misplaced, and the bountiful blind woman
doth most mistake in her gifts to women.   35

Cel. 'Tis true; for those that she makes fair she
scarce makes honest, and those that she makes honest
she makes very ill-favoredly.

Ros. Nay, now thou goest from Fortune's office to
Nature's. Fortune reigns in gifts of the world, not in   40
the lineaments of Nature.

Enter [*Touchstone, the*] *Clown.*

Cel. No? When Nature hath made a fair creature,
may she not by Fortune fall into the fire? Though
Nature hath given us wit to flout at Fortune, hath not
Fortune sent in this fool to cut off the argument?   45

Ros. Indeed, there is Fortune too hard for Nature
when Fortune makes Nature's natural the cutter-off
of Nature's wit.

53-4. How now, wit? Whither wander you: a proverbial saying addressed to anyone whose speech was becoming too fantastic, but here also used as a greeting to Touchstone.

63. naught: worthless.

65. forsworn: perjured.

Cel. Peradventure this is not Fortune's work neither, but Nature's, who perceiving our natural wits 50 too dull to reason of such goddesses, hath sent this natural for our whetstone, for always the dullness of the fool is the whetstone of the wits. How now, wit? Whither wander you?

Touch. Mistress, you must come away to your fa- 55 ther.

Cel. Were you made the messenger?

Touch. No, by mine honor, but I was bid to come for you.

Ros. Where learned you that oath, fool? 60

Touch. Of a certain knight that swore by his honor they were good pancakes, and swore by his honor the mustard was naught. Now I'll stand to it, the pancakes were naught, and the mustard was good, and yet was not the knight forsworn. 65

Cel. How prove you that in the great heap of your knowledge?

Ros. Ay, marry, now unmuzzle your wisdom.

Touch. Stand you both forth now. Stroke your chins, and swear by your beards that I am a knave. 70

Cel. By our beards (if we had them), thou art.

Touch. By my knavery (if I had it), then I were. But if you swear by that that is not, you are not forsworn. No more was this knight, swearing by his honor, for he never had any; or if he had, he had 75 sworn it away before ever he saw those pancakes or that mustard.

Cel. Prithee, who is't that thou meanst?

Touch. One that old Frederick, your father, loves.

80. **Cel.:** This speech is given to Rosalind in the Folios, but editors have generally agreed with Lewis Theobald's suggestion that the speaker should be Celia.

82. **taxation:** that is, for being too critical of his betters.

97. **color:** kind. Le Beau takes the question literally and is at a loss to answer truthfully.

103. **if I keep not my rank:** Touchstone was presumably about to refer to maintaining his usual standard of wit.

Cel. My father's love is enough to honor him. 80
Enough! Speak no more of him. You'll be whipped
for taxation one of these days.

Touch. The more pity that fools may not speak
wisely what wise men do foolishly.

Cel. By my troth, thou sayest true; for, since the 85
little wit that fools have was silenced, the little foolery
that wise men have makes a great show. Here comes
Monsieur Le Beau.

Enter *Le Beau.*

Ros. With his mouth full of news.

Cel. Which he will put on us as pigeons feed their 90
young.

Ros. Then shall we be news-crammed.

Cel. All the better! We shall be the more market-
able.—Bon jour, Monsieur Le Beau. What's the news?

Le Beau. Fair princess, you have lost much good 95
sport.

Cel. Sport? of what color?

Le Beau. What color, madam? How shall I answer
you?

Ros. As wit and fortune will.   100

Touch. Or as the Destinies decree.

Cel. Well said! That was laid on with a trowel.

Touch. Nay, if I keep not my rank—

Ros. Thou losest thy old smell.

Le Beau. You amaze me, ladies. I would have told 105
you of good wrestling, which you have lost the sight
of.

117. **proper:** handsome, fine.

126. **dole:** lamentation.

136-37. **broken music:** a pun. **Broken music** was a term applied to music arranged for or played by several different instruments as opposed, for example, to a matched set of instruments of one kind.

Ros. Yet tell us the manner of the wrestling.

Le Beau. I will tell you the beginning; and if it please your ladyships, you may see the end, for the 110 best is yet to do; and here, where you are, they are coming to perform it.

Cel. Well, the beginning that is dead and buried.

Le Beau. There comes an old man and his three sons— 115

Cel. I could match this beginning with an old tale.

Le Beau. Three proper young men, of excellent growth and presence.

Ros. With bills on their necks, "Be it known unto all men by these presents"— 120

Le Beau. The eldest of the three wrestled with Charles, the Duke's wrestler; which Charles in a moment threw him and broke three of his ribs, that there is little hope of life in him. So he served the second, and so the third. Yonder they lie, the poor old man, 125 their father, making such pitiful dole over them that all the beholders take his part with weeping.

Ros. Alas!

Touch. But what is the sport, monsieur, that the ladies have lost? 130

Le Beau. Why, this that I speak of.

Touch. Thus men may grow wiser every day. It is the first time that ever I heard breaking of ribs was sport for ladies.

Cel. Or I, I promise thee. 135

Ros. But is there any else longs to see this broken music in his sides? Is there yet another dotes upon rib-breaking? Shall we see this wrestling, cousin?

145. **his own peril on his forwardness:** i.e., let his danger be blamed on his own presumption.

148-49. **successfully:** that is, as if he could be successful.

152. **so please you give us leave:** if it please you to allow us.

154. **there is such odds in the man:** that is, Orlando is obviously no match for Charles.

155. **fain:** like to.

162. **them:** perhaps Orlando uses the plural because he does not know which lady is the princess and therefore includes them both.

Le Beau. You must, if you stay here; for here is the
place appointed for the wrestling, and they are ready   140
to perform it.

Cel. Yonder sure they are coming. Let us now stay
and see it.

*Flourish. Enter Duke [Frederick], Lords, Orlando,
Charles, and Attendants.*

Duke. Come on. Since the youth will not be entreated, his own peril on his forwardness!   145

Ros. Is yonder the man?

Le Beau. Even he, madam.

Cel. Alas, he is too young! Yet he looks successfully.

Duke. How now, daughter, and cousin! Are you   150
crept hither to see the wrestling?

Ros. Ay, my liege, so please you give us leave.

Duke. You will take little delight in it, I can tell
you, there is such odds in the man. In pity of the challenger's youth I would fain dissuade him, but he will   155
not be entreated. Speak to him, ladies; see if you can
move him.

Cel. Call him hither, good Monsieur Le Beau.

Duke. Do so. I'll not be by.   [*Moves away.*]

Le Beau. Monsieur the challenger, the princess   160
calls for you.

Orl. I attend them with all respect and duty.

Ros. Young man, have you challenged Charles the
wrestler?

Orl. No, fair princess. He is the general challenger;   165

176. **misprized:** undervalued; see I. i. 162.
182. **foiled:** beaten; see I. i. 124.
183. **gracious:** graced, honored; see I. i. 142.
186. **Only in the world:** i.e., the fact is that I only fill up a space in the world.
192-93. **be deceived in:** underestimate.

I come but in as others do, to try with him the
strength of my youth.

Cel. Young gentleman, your spirits are too bold for
your years. You have seen cruel proof of this man's
strength. If you saw yourself with your eyes, or knew 170
yourself with your judgment, the fear of your adventure would counsel you to a more equal enterprise.
We pray you for your own sake to embrace your own
safety and give over this attempt.

Ros. Do, young sir. Your reputation shall not there- 175
fore be misprized. We will make it our suit to the
Duke that the wrestling might not go forward.

Orl. I beseech you, punish me not with your hard
thoughts, wherein I confess me much guilty to deny
so fair and excellent ladies anything. But let your fair 180
eyes and gentle wishes go with me to my trial; wherein if I be foiled, there is but one shamed that was
never gracious; if killed, but one dead that is willing
to be so. I shall do my friends no wrong, for I have
none to lament me; the world no injury, for in it I 185
have nothing. Only in the world I fill up a place,
which may be better supplied when I have made it
empty.

Ros. The little strength that I have, I would it were
with you.   190

Cel. And mine, to eke out hers.

Ros. Fare you well. Pray heaven I be deceived in
you!

Cel. Your heart's desires be with you!

Cha. Come, where is this young gallant that is so 195
desirous to lie with his mother earth?

204. **come your ways:** come on; let's go.
205. **be thy speed:** aid you.
223. **still:** always.

Orl. Ready, sir; but his will hath in it a more
modest working.

Duke. You shall try but one fall.

Cha. No, I warrant your Grace you shall not en-   200
treat him to a second that have so mightily per-
suaded him from a first.

Orl. You mean to mock me after. You should not
have mocked me before. But come your ways!

Ros. Now Hercules be thy speed, young man!   205

Cel. I would I were invisible, to catch the strong
fellow by the leg.   *Wrestle.*

Ros. O excellent young man!

Cel. If I had a thunderbolt in mine eye, I can tell
who should down.   210

                [*Charles is thrown.*] *Shout.*

Duke. No more, no more!

Orl. Yes, I beseech your Grace. I am not yet well
breathed.

Duke. How dost thou, Charles?

Le Beau. He cannot speak, my lord.   215

Duke. Bear him away. [*Charles is borne out.*]
What is thy name, young man?

Orl. Orlando, my liege, the youngest son of Sir
Rowland de Boys.

Duke. I would thou hadst been son to some man 220
    else!

The world esteemed thy father honorable,
But I did find him still mine enemy.

Thou shouldst have better pleased me with this deed,
Hadst thou descended from another house.   225

235. **unto:** in addition to.

239. **envious:** malicious; see I. i. 137.

242. **But justly as you have exceeded all promise:** exactly as well as your performance has exceeded your promise as a wrestler.

245. **out of suits with Fortune:** whose suits to Fortune go unheeded.

246. **could:** i.e., would willingly.

251. **quintain:** a post used as a mark in tilting or other military exercise.

But fare thee well; thou art a gallant youth;
I would thou hadst told me of another father.

Exeunt Duke, [Train, and Le Beau].

Cel. Were I my father, coz, would I do this?

Orl. I am more proud to be Sir Rowland's son,
His youngest son, and would not change that calling 230
To be adopted heir to Frederick.

Ros. My father loved Sir Rowland as his soul,
And all the world was of my father's mind.
Had I before known this young man his son,
I should have given him tears unto entreaties   235
Ere he should thus have ventured.

Cel.   Gentle cousin,
Let us go thank him and encourage him.
My father's rough and envious disposition
Sticks me at heart. Sir, you have well deserved.   240
If you do keep your promises in love
But justly as you have exceeded all promise,
Your mistress shall be happy.

Ros.   Gentleman,

[*Giving him a chain from her neck*]

Wear this for me, one out of suits with Fortune,   245
That could give more but that her hand lacks means.
Shall we go, coz?

Cel.   Ay. Fare you well, fair gentleman.

Orl. Can I not say "I thank you"? My better parts
Are all thrown down, and that which here stands up 250
Is but a quintain, a mere lifeless block.

Ros. He calls us back. My pride fell with my for-
         tunes;
I'll ask him what he would. Did you call, sir?

258. **Have with you:** I'm ready, let's go.

261. **urged conference:** offered conversation.

263. **Or:** either.

265. **Albeit:** although.

268. **misconsters:** misconstrues, distorts.

269. **humorous:** capricious.

270. **More suits you to conceive than I to speak of:** can more fittingly be imagined by you than expressed by myself.

276. **smaller:** "taller" in the Folios; Edmund Malone's correction.

279. **whose loves:** that is, love for each other.

Sir, you have wrestled well, and overthrown   255
More than your enemies.
   Cel.   Will you go, coz?
   Ros. Have with you. Fare you well.
                  Exeunt [Rosalind and Celia].
   Orl. What passion hangs these weights upon my
    tongue?   260
I cannot speak to her, yet she urged conference.

          [Re-]enter *Le Beau*.

O poor Orlando, thou art overthrown!
Or Charles or something weaker masters thee.
   Le Beau. Good sir, I do in friendship counsel you
To leave this place. Albeit you have deserved   265
High commendation, true applause, and love,
Yet such is now the Duke's condition
That he misconsters all that you have done.
The Duke is humorous. What he is, indeed,
More suits you to conceive than I to speak of.   270
   Orl. I thank you, sir: and pray you tell me this—
Which of the two was daughter of the Duke,
That here was at the wrestling?
   Le Beau. Neither his daughter, if we judge by man-
    ners;   275
But yet indeed the smaller is his daughter;
The other is daughter to the banished Duke,
And here detained by her usurping uncle
To keep his daughter company, whose loves
Are dearer than the natural bond of sisters.   280

283. **argument:** reason; see I. ii. 45.
290. **rest:** remain.

━━━━━━━━━━━━━━━━━━━━━━━━━━━━━━

I. iii. Celia is teasing Rosalind about her obvious interest in Orlando when her father enters and orders Rosalind to leave the court at once on pain of death. Celia is loyal to her cousin and determines to go with her. They agree to set out for the Forest of Arden to seek Rosalind's father. For greater safety Rosalind will assume masculine dress and they will take Touchstone to console them in their travels.

━━━━━━━━━━━━━━━━━━━━━━━━

3. **Not one to throw at a dog:** proverbial: not one word if her life depended on it.
9. **mad:** despondent, melancholy.

But I can tell you that of late this Duke
Hath ta'en displeasure 'gainst his gentle niece,
Grounded upon no other argument
But that the people praise her for her virtues
And pity her for her good father's sake;   285
And, on my life, his malice 'gainst the lady
Will suddenly break forth. Sir, fare you well.
Hereafter, in a better world than this,
I shall desire more love and knowledge of you.

Orl. I rest much bounden to you. Fare you well. 290
                              [*Exit Le Beau.*]
Thus must I from the smoke into the smother,
From tyrant Duke unto a tyrant brother.
But heavenly Rosalind!

                                               Exit.

Scene III. [A room in the Palace.]

Enter *Celia* and *Rosalind*.

Cel. Why, cousin! why, Rosalind! Cupid have
mercy! not a word?

Ros. Not one to throw at a dog.

Cel. No, thy words are too precious to be cast away
upon curs; throw some of them at me. Come, lame me   5
with reasons.

Ros. Then there were two cousins laid up, when
the one should be lamed with reasons, and the other
mad without any.

Cel. But is all this for your father?   10

11. **child's father:** future husband, i.e., Orlando, with whom she is hopelessly in love. The poet Samuel Taylor Coleridge objected to this phrase on the grounds that it was "a most indelicate anticipation" to attribute to Rosalind. Nicholas Rowe and some other editors preferred to alter the reading to "father's child."

19-20. **cry "hem!" and have him:** have him for the asking.

25-6. **turning these jests out of service:** i.e., dismissing them, as one might a servant.

30. **ensue:** follow as a matter of course.

31. **By this kind of chase:** pursuing this train of logic.

32. **dearly:** bitterly, intensely.

35. **deserve well:** well deserve to be hated, since his father was the enemy of mine.

Ros. No, some of it is for my child's father. O, how full of briers is this working-day world!

Cel. They are but burrs, cousin, thrown upon thee in holiday foolery. If we walk not in the trodden paths, our very petticoats will catch them.   15

Ros. I could shake them off my coat. These burrs are in my heart.

Cel. Hem them away.

Ros. I would try, if I could cry "hem!" and have him.   20

Cel. Come, come, wrestle with thy affections.

Ros. O, they take the part of a better wrestler than myself!

Cel. O, a good wish upon you! You will try in time, in despite of a fall. But, turning these jests out of   25 service, let us talk in good earnest. Is it possible on such a sudden you should fall into so strong a liking with old Sir Rowland's youngest son?

Ros. The Duke my father loved his father dearly.

Cel. Doth it therefore ensue that you should love   30 his son dearly? By this kind of chase, I should hate him, for my father hated his father dearly; yet I hate not Orlando.

Ros. No, faith, hate him not, for my sake!

Cel. Why should I not? Doth he not deserve well?   35

Enter *Duke* [*Frederick*], with *Lords*.

Ros. Let me love him for that; and do you love him because I do. Look, here comes the Duke.

Cel. With his eyes full of anger.

39. **your safest haste:** i.e., the faster the better for your safety.

42. **cousin:** a term of kinship used loosely to most near relatives.

48. **hold intelligence:** have discourse; i.e., if I am on speaking terms with myself.

55. **purgation:** clearance.

56. **Grace:** Divine Grace.

Duke. Mistress, dispatch you with your safest haste
And get you from our court!   40

Ros.   Me, uncle!

Duke.   You, cousin.
Within these ten days if that thou beest found
So near our public court as twenty miles,
Thou diest for it.   45

Ros.   I do beseech your Grace
Let me the knowledge of my fault bear with me.
If with myself I hold intelligence
Or have acquaintance with mine own desires;
If that I do not dream or be not frantic,   50
As I do trust I am not—then, dear uncle,
Never so much as in a thought unborn
Did I offend your Highness.

Duke.   Thus do all traitors.
If their purgation did consist in words,
They are as innocent as Grace itself.   55
Let it suffice thee that I trust thee not.

Ros. Yet your mistrust cannot make me a traitor.
Tell me whereon the likelihood depends.

Duke. Thou art thy father's daughter. There's   60
     enough!

Ros. So was I when your Highness took his duke-
     dom;
So was I when your Highness banished him.
Treason is not inherited, my lord;   65
Or if we did derive it from our friends,
What's that to me? My father was no traitor.
Then, good my liege, mistake me not so much
To think my poverty is treacherous.

Venus with her swans.
From Vincenzo Cartari, *Le vere e nove Imagini de gli dei delli antichi* (1615).

77. **still:** always; see I. ii. 223.

79. **Juno's swans:** Shakespeare's memory failed him here. A pair of swans (sometimes doves) were supposed to draw Venus' chariot. No allusion has been found in mythology to connect swans with Juno.

95. **in the greatness of my word:** on my word as a mighty ruler.

Cel. Dear sovereign, hear me speak.   70
Duke. Ay, Celia. We stayed her for your sake,
Else had she with her father ranged along.
Cel. I did not then entreat to have her stay;
It was your pleasure and your own remorse.
I was too young that time to value her;   75
But now I know her. If she be a traitor,
Why, so am I! We still have slept together,
Rose at an instant, learned, played, eat together;
And wheresoe'er we went, like Juno's swans,
Still we went coupled and inseparable.   80
Duke. She is too subtle for thee; and her smooth-
          ness,
Her very silence and her patience,
Speak to the people, and they pity her.
Thou art a fool. She robs thee of thy name,   85
And thou wilt show more bright and seem more virtu-
          ous
When she is gone. Then open not thy lips.
Firm and irrevocable is my doom
Which I have passed upon her. She is banished.   90
Cel. Pronounce that sentence then on me, my liege!
I cannot live out of her company.
Duke. You are a fool. You, niece, provide yourself.
If you outstay the time, upon mine honor,
And in the greatness of my word, you die.   95
                    Exeunt Duke &c.
Cel. O my poor Rosalind! whither wilt thou go?
Wilt thou change fathers? I will give thee mine.
I charge thee be not thou more grieved than I am.
Ros. I have more cause.

120. **umber:** brown earth.

125. **suit me all points:** attire myself completely, from head to toe.

126. **curtleaxe:** cutlass.

129. **swashing:** swashbuckling, swaggering.

Cel.   Thou hast not, cousin.   100
Prithee be cheerful. Knowst thou not the Duke
Hath banished me, his daughter?
    Ros.   That he hath not!
    Cel. No? hath not? Rosalind lacks then the love
Which teacheth me that thou and I am one.   105
Shall we be sund'red? shall we part, sweet girl?
No! let my father seek another heir.
Therefore devise with me how we may fly,
Whither to go, and what to bear with us.
And do not seek to take your charge upon you,   110
To bear your griefs yourself and leave me out;
For, by this heaven, now at our sorrows pale,
Say what thou canst, I'll go along with thee!
    Ros. Why, whither shall we go?
    Cel. To seek my uncle in the Forest of Arden.   115
    Ros. Alas, what danger will it be to us,
Maids as we are, to travel forth so far!
Beauty provoketh thieves sooner than gold.
    Cel. I'll put myself in poor and mean attire
And with a kind of umber smirch my face;   120
The like do you. So shall we pass along
And never stir assailants.
    Ros.   Were it not better,
Because that I am more than common tall,
That I did suit me all points like a man?   125
A gallant curtleaxe upon my thigh,
A boar-spear in my hand, and—in my heart
Lie there what hidden woman's fear there will—
We'll have a swashing and a martial outside,

The rape of Ganymede.
From Gabriel Simeoni, *La vita et Metamorfoseo d'Ovidio* (1559).

131. outface it with their semblances: carry it off with their appearances of bravery.

135. Ganymede: a beautiful boy, kidnaped by Jove to be his cupbearer.

As many other mannish cowards have   130
That do outface it with their semblances.

   Cel. What shall I call thee when thou art a man?

   Ros. I'll have no worse a name than Jove's own
     page,
And therefore look you call me Ganymede.   135
But what will you be called?

   Cel. Something that hath a reference to my state—
No longer Celia, but Aliena.

   Ros. But, cousin, what if we assayed to steal
The clownish fool out of your father's court?   140
Would he not be a comfort to our travel?

   Cel. He'll go along o'er the wide world with me.
Leave me alone to woo him. Let's away
And get our jewels and our wealth together,
Devise the fittest time and safest way   145
To hide us from pursuit that will be made
After my flight. Now go we in content
To liberty, and not to banishment.

                       Exeunt.

AS YOU LIKE IT

ACT II

Seeking a toadstone.
From *Hortus sanitatis* (1536).

II. i. Duke Senior, Rosalind's father, is introduced in his forest paradise. The Duke is philosophical about his exile and points out to his companions the advantages of the simple life they lead compared with that of the sophisticated court. Only one of the company, the melancholy Jaques, is reported to be distressed at their despoiling of the wilderness in order to live.

7. **chiding:** scolding.

11. **feelingly:** i.e., by means of my senses, with a pun on "earnestly," "eagerly."

14. **yet:** nevertheless; **a precious jewel:** i.e., his brilliant eyes (in contrast to his general ugliness) and the toadstone, popularly believed to be found in a toad's head and to be a powerful protection against poison (in contrast to the "venomous" effect of the toad himself—an erroneous belief of the time). Shakespeare possibly had both ideas in mind.

15. **exempt from public haunt:** free of contact with the mass of mankind.

ACT II

Scene I. [The Forest of Arden.]

Enter *Duke Senior*, *Amiens*, and two or three *Lords*,
like *Foresters*.

Duke S. Now, my co-mates and brothers in exile,
Hath not old custom made this life more sweet
Than that of painted pomp? Are not these woods
More free from peril than the envious court?
Here feel we but the penalty of Adam,   5
The seasons' difference; as, the icy fang
And churlish chiding of the winter's wind,
Which, when it bites and blows upon my body
Even till I shrink with cold, I smile, and say
"This is no flattery; these are counselors   10
That feelingly persuade me what I am."
Sweet are the uses of adversity,
Which, like the toad, ugly and venomous,
Wears yet a precious jewel in his head;
And this our life, exempt from public haunt,   15
Finds tongues in trees, books in the running brooks,
Sermons in stones, and good in everything:
I would not change it.

20. **stubbornness:** perversity; see I. i. 135-36, **stubbornest.**

23. **fools:** simple creatures. The word was often used as a term expressing pity or fondness.

24. **burghers:** citizens, inhabitants.

25. **forked heads:** i.e., the barbed heads of arrows, which are compared to the antlered heads of the male deer themselves.

28. **melancholy:** contemplative; given to whimsical moods.

29. **in that kind:** that is, by so doing (shooting deer).

35. **sequestered:** cut off from his kind.

43. **of:** by.

49. **needless:** i.e., unneedy, having all the water it needed.

Closing in on the deer.
From George Turberville, *The Noble Art of Venery or Hunting* (1575).

Ami.   Happy is your Grace
That can translate the stubbornness of fortune   20
Into so quiet and so sweet a style.
   Duke S. Come, shall we go and kill us venison?
And yet it irks me the poor dappled fools,
Being native burghers of this desert city,
Should, in their own confines, with forked heads   25
Have their round haunches gored.
   1. Lord.   Indeed, my lord,
The melancholy Jaques grieves at that,
And in that kind swears you do more usurp
Than doth your brother that hath banished you.   30
Today my Lord of Amiens and myself
Did steal behind him as he lay along
Under an oak, whose antique root peeps out
Upon the brook that brawls along this wood;
To the which place a poor sequestered stag,   35
That from the hunter's aim had ta'en a hurt,
Did come to languish; and indeed, my lord,
The wretched animal heaved forth such groans
That their discharge did stretch his leathern coat
Almost to bursting, and the big round tears   40
Coursed one another down his innocent nose
In piteous chase; and thus the hairy fool,
Much marked of the melancholy Jaques,
Stood on the extremest verge of the swift brook,
Augmenting it with tears.   45
   Duke S.   But what said Jaques?
Did he not moralize this spectacle?
   1. Lord. O, yes, into a thousand similes.
First, for his weeping into the needless stream:

50. **testament:** will.

52. **Then, being alone:** i.e., on the subject of its being alone.

54-5. **misery doth part/ The flux of company:** misery sets one apart from the flood of company; **Anon:** at once.

59. **Wherefore do you look:** why do you look; what profit is there in it for you to so much as notice him.

61. **invectively:** with harsh criticism.

64. **mere:** unqualified, absolute; **tyrants:** synonymous with **usurpers; what's worse:** whatever worse term one can think of.

65. **kill them up:** kill them off; destroy them completely so as to wipe them out.

72. **cope:** encounter; **sullen:** moody.

73. **matter:** i.e., food for thought.

74. **straight:** immediately.

The kill.
From George Turberville, *The Noble Art of Venery or Hunting* (1575).

"Poor deer," quoth he, "thou makest a testament   50
As worldlings do, giving thy sum of more
To that which had too much." Then, being alone,
Left and abandoned of his velvet friends:
"'Tis right!" quoth he, "thus misery doth part
The flux of company." Anon a careless herd,   55
Full of the pasture, jumps along by him
And never stays to greet him: "Ay," quoth Jaques,
"Sweep on, you fat and greasy citizens!
'Tis just the fashion! Wherefore do you look
Upon that poor and broken bankrupt there?"   60
Thus most invectively he pierceth through
The body of the country, city, court;
Yea, and of this our life, swearing that we
Are mere usurpers, tyrants, and what's worse,
To fright the animals and to kill them up   65
In their assigned and native dwelling place.
   Duke S. And did you leave him in this contempla-
     tion?
   2. Lord. We did, my lord, weeping and commenting
Upon the sobbing deer.   70
   Duke S.   Show me the place.
I love to cope him in these sullen fits,
For then he's full of matter.
   1. Lord. I'll bring you to him straight.

                        Exeunt.

II. ii. The Duke has learned that Celia has left with Rosalind and gives orders that they be brought back. He is told that the clown is also missing and that the cousins had been much taken with Orlando, who may have helped them. The Duke commands that Oliver be brought to him to answer for his brother if Orlando cannot be found.

▬▬▬▬▬▬▬▬▬▬▬▬

3. **Are of consent and sufferance in this:** have approved this and made it possible.

8. **roynish:** contemptible; literally, "mangy."

13. **parts and graces:** physical characteristics and abilities.

20. **inquisition:** questioning; **quail:** falter.

Scene II. [A room in the Palace.]

Enter *Duke* [*Frederick*], with *Lords*.

Duke. Can it be possible that no man saw them?
It cannot be. Some villains of my court
Are of consent and sufferance in this.

1. Lord. I cannot hear of any that did see her.
The ladies her attendants of her chamber   5
Saw her abed, and in the morning early
They found the bed untreasured of their mistress.

2. Lord. My lord, the roynish clown at whom so oft
Your Grace was wont to laugh is also missing.
Hisperia, the princess' gentlewoman,   10
Confesses that she secretly o'erheard
Your daughter and her cousin much commend
The parts and graces of the wrestler
That did but lately foil the sinewy Charles,
And she believes, wherever they are gone,   15
That youth is surely in their company.

Duke. Send to his brother, fetch that gallant hither.
If he be absent, bring his brother to me;
I'll make him find him. Do this suddenly,
And let not search and inquisition quail   20
To bring again these foolish runaways.

Exeunt.

II. iii. Adam, the devoted old servant of Orlando and his father, warns Orlando that Oliver's jealous hatred has reached such a height that he plans to kill him by one means or another. Orlando points out that if he leaves his brother's home he has no means of support except to beg or steal, courses which his honor forbids, but Adam offers him his life savings of five hundred crowns. Orlando is heartened by the old man's devotion and they agree to seek their fortunes together elsewhere.

<hr>

4. **memory:** i.e., reminder, because resembling him so much.

5. **what make you here:** what are you doing here—this is no place for you.

8. **fond:** foolish; **to:** as to.

9. **bonny:** stalwart, of impressive physique; **prizer:** champion wrestler; **humorous:** capricious; see I. ii. 269.

13. **No more:** i.e., no better.

15. **comely:** becoming, attractive. Shakespeare probably remembers the story of the handsome but envenomed garment which Nessus tricked Deianira into giving to Hercules, as told in Ovid, *Metamorphoses*, Book 9.

Scene III. [Before Oliver's house.]

Enter Orlando *and* Adam, *[from opposite directions].*

    Orl. Who's there?
    Adam. What, my young master! O my gentle mas-
    ter!
O my sweet master! O you memory
Of old Sir Rowland! Why, what make you here?   5
Why are you virtuous? Why do people love you?
And wherefore are you gentle, strong, and valiant?
Why would you be so fond to overcome
The bonny prizer of the humorous Duke?
Your praise is come too swiftly home before you.   10
Know you not, master, to some kind of men
Their graces serve them but as enemies?
No more do yours. Your virtues, gentle master,
Are sanctified and holy traitors to you.
O, what a world is this, when what is comely   15
Envenoms him that bears it!
    Orl. Why, what's the matter?
    Adam.   O unhappy youth,
Come not within these doors! Within this roof
The enemy of all your graces lives.   20
Your brother (no, no brother! yet the son—
Yet not the son—I will not call him son
Of him I was about to call his father)
Hath heard your praises, and this night he means
To burn the lodging where you use to lie   25
And you within it. If he fail of that,

28. **practices:** plots; see I. i. 143.
29. **butchery:** slaughterhouse.
30. **Abhor:** recoil in horror from—a physical act, not a mere emotional reaction.
36. **boisterous:** violent.
41. **diverted:** alienated.
46. **unregarded age in corners thrown:** that is, himself, an unvalued old man, be discarded as of no further use.
49. **Be comfort to:** strengthen, invigorate.
53. **rebellious:** i.e., destructive of natural health.

He will have other means to cut you off.
I overheard him and his practices.
This is no place, this house is but a butchery.
Abhor it, fear it, do not enter it!   30
   Orl. Why, whither, Adam, wouldst thou have me
    go?
   Adam. No matter whither, so you come not here.
   Orl. What, wouldst thou have me go and beg my
    food,   35
Or with a base and boisterous sword enforce
A thievish living on the common road?
This I must do, or know not what to do.
Yet this I will not do, do how I can.
I rather will subject me to the malice   40
Of a diverted blood and bloody brother.
   Adam. But do not so. I have five hundred crowns,
The thrifty hire I saved under your father,
Which I did store to be my foster nurse
When service should in my old limbs lie lame   45
And unregarded age in corners thrown.
Take that, and He that doth the ravens feed,
Yea, providently caters for the sparrow,
Be comfort to my age! Here is the gold;
All this I give you. Let me be your servant.   50
Though I look old, yet I am strong and lusty;
For in my youth I never did apply
Hot and rebellious liquors in my blood,
Nor did not with unbashful forehead woo
The means of weakness and debility;   55
Therefore my age is as a lusty winter,
Frosty, but kindly. Let me go with you;

61. **constant:** faithful.

62. **meed:** wages, compensation.

65-6. **choke their service up/ Even with the having:** that is, cut off their service as soon as they have gained the material advantage they sought.

67. **prunest:** i.e., attempt to doctor.

72. **some settled low content:** a humble manner of living which will content us.

75. **seventeen:** Rowe's suggestion; the Folios read "seventy."

78. **too late a week:** equivalent to the modern expression "too late a day."

I'll do the service of a younger man
In all your business and necessities.

  Orl. O good old man, how well in thee appears   60
The constant service of the antique world,
When service sweat for duty, not for meed!
Thou art not for the fashion of these times,
Where none will sweat but for promotion,
And having that, do choke their service up   65
Even with the having. It is not so with thee.
But, poor old man, thou prunest a rotten tree
That cannot so much as a blossom yield
In lieu of all thy pains and husbandry.
But come thy ways! We'll go along together,   70
And ere we have thy youthful wages spent,
We'll light upon some settled low content.

  Adam. Master, go on, and I will follow thee
To the last gasp with truth and loyalty!
From seventeen years till now almost fourscore   75
Here lived I, but now live here no more.
At seventeen years many their fortunes seek,
But at fourscore it is too late a week;
Yet fortune cannot recompense me better
Than to die well and not my master's debtor.   80

                    Exeunt.

II. iv. Rosalind, Celia, and Touchstone come upon Corin, a shepherd, in the Forest of Arden. Learning that a nearby cottage with flocks and pasture is to be sold by Corin's master, Rosalind commissions Corin to buy them for their company.

⁙⁙⁙⁙⁙⁙⁙⁙⁙⁙⁙⁙⁙⁙⁙⁙⁙⁙⁙⁙

6. **doublet and hose:** the contemporary male costume of a close-fitting jacket, and short breeches supplemented by long stockings.

12. **cross:** a pun on **cross** (vexation) and **cross** (a coin stamped with a cross).

17. **must be content:** must be patient with the inconveniences they suffer.

Scene IV. [Another part of the Forest of Arden.]

Enter *Rosalind* for *Ganymede*, *Celia* for *Aliena*, and
Clown, alias *Touchstone*.

Ros. O Jupiter, how weary are my spirits!

Touch. I care not for my spirits if my legs were not
weary.

Ros. I could find in my heart to disgrace my man's
apparel and to cry like a woman; but I must comfort 5
the weaker vessel, as doublet and hose ought to show
itself courageous to petticoat. Therefore, courage,
good Aliena!

Cel. I pray you bear with me; I cannot go no further. 10

Touch. For my part, I had rather bear with you
than bear you. Yet I should bear no cross if I did bear
you, for I think you have no money in your purse.

Ros. Well, this is the Forest of Arden.

Touch. Ay, now am I in Arden, the more fool I! 15
When I was at home, I was in a better place; but
travelers must be content.

Enter *Corin* and *Silvius*.

Ros. Ay, be so, good Touchstone.—Look you, who
comes here,

A young man and an old in solemn talk. 20

Cor. That is the way to make her scorn you still.

Sil. O Corin, that thou knewst how I do love her!

30. **fantasy:** fancy; i.e., both "imagination" and "love."

40. **passion:** strong emotion.

43. **hard adventure:** a stroke of bad luck.

47. **batlet:** a wooden paddle used by washwomen for beating clothes.

48. **chopt:** chapped.

49. **peascod:** peapod.

52-3. **as all is mortal in nature, so is all nature in love mortal in folly:** as all humanity is mortal, so is the folly caused by love a sign of humanity.

From Pietro de Crescenzi, *Nel quale si trattano gli ordini di tutte le cose che si appartengono a commodi e a gli utili della villa* (1561).

Cor. I partly guess; for I have loved ere now.

Sil. No, Corin, being old, thou canst not guess,
Though in thy youth thou wast as true a lover   25
As ever sighed upon a midnight pillow.
But if thy love were ever like to mine
(As sure I think did never man love so),
How many actions most ridiculous
Hast thou been drawn to by thy fantasy!   30

Cor. Into a thousand that I have forgotten.

Sil. O, thou didst then never love so heartily!
If thou rememb'rest not the slightest folly
That ever love did make thee run into,
Thou hast not loved.   35
Or if thou hast not sat as I do now,
Wearing thy hearer in thy mistress' praise,
Thou hast not loved.
Or if thou hast not broke from company
Abruptly, as my passion now makes me,   40
Thou hast not loved. O Phebe, Phebe, Phebe!   *Exit.*

Ros. Alas, poor shepherd! Searching of thy wound,
I have by hard adventure found mine own.

Touch. And I mine. I remember, when I was in love
I broke my sword upon a stone and bid him take that   45
for coming a-night to Jane Smile; and I remember the
kissing of her batlet, and the cow's dugs that her
pretty chopt hands had milked; and I remember the
wooing of a peascod instead of her, from whom I took
two cods, and giving her them again, said with weep-   50
ing tears, "Wear these for my sake." We that are true
lovers run into strange capers; but as all is mortal in
nature, so is all nature in love mortal in folly.

55. **wit:** wisdom.

59. **something:** somewhat.

64. **clown:** the city dweller's term for a country-man.

81. **churlish:** miserly.

82. **little recks to find:** sets little store by finding.

84. **cote:** cottage; **bounds of feed:** i.e., his holdings of pasture land.

From *Hortus sanitatis* (1536).

Ros. Thou speakst wiser than thou art ware of.

Touch. Nay, I shall ne'er be ware of mine own wit   55
till I break my shins against it.

Ros. Jove, Jove! this shepherd's passion
Is much upon my fashion.

Touch. And mine, but it grows something stale
with me.   60

Cel. I pray you, one of you question yond man
If he for gold will give us any food.
I faint almost to death.

Touch.   Holla, you clown!

Ros. Peace, fool! he's not thy kinsman.   65

Cor.   Who calls?

Touch. Your betters, sir.

Cor.   Else are they very wretched.

Ros. Peace, I say!—Good even to you, friend.

Cor. And to you, gentle sir, and to you all.   70

Ros. I prithee, shepherd, if that love or gold
Can in this desert place buy entertainment,
Bring us where we may rest ourselves and feed.
Here's a young maid with travel much oppressed,
And faints for succor.   75

Cor.   Fair sir, I pity her
And wish, for her sake more than for mine own,
My fortunes were more able to relieve her;
But I am shepherd to another man
And do not shear the fleeces that I graze.   80
My master is of churlish disposition
And little recks to find the way to heaven
By doing deeds of hospitality.
Besides, his cote, his flocks, and bounds of feed

88. **in my voice:** as far as my authority extends.

91-2. **but erewhile:** just a while ago.

94. **if it stand with honesty:** if it will be honorable.

96. **have to pay for it of us:** i.e., we will pay you for it.

97. **mend:** improve.

98. **waste:** spend, while away.

102. **feeder:** i.e., one who depends on you: a servant.

<hr>

II. v. The melancholy Jaques gives Amiens, of Duke Senior's company, a taste of his philosophy.

<hr>

3-4. **turn his merry note/ Unto the sweet bird's throat:** i.e., imitate the warbling of the birds. The repetition of "Come hither" may be a verbalization of a particular bird's song.

Are now on sale, and at our sheepcote now,   85
By reason of his absence, there is nothing
That you will feed on; but what is, come see,
And in my voice most welcome shall you be.
   Ros. What is he that shall buy his flock and pas-
     ture?   90
   Cor. That young swain that you saw here but ere-
     while,
That little cares for buying anything.
   Ros. I pray thee, if it stand with honesty,
Buy thou the cottage, pasture, and the flock,   95
And thou shalt have to pay for it of us.
   Cel. And we will mend thy wages. I like this place
And willingly could waste my time in it.
   Cor. Assuredly the thing is to be sold.
Go with me. If you like, upon report,   100
The soil, the profit, and this kind of life,
I will your very faithful feeder be
And buy it with your gold right suddenly.

                                 Exeunt.

Scene V. [Another part of the Forest.]

Enter *Amiens, Jaques,* and others.

Song.

   Ami. Under the greenwood tree
       Who loves to lie with me,
       And turn his merry note

17. **stanzo:** stanza, verse.

20-1. **I care not for their names; they owe me nothing:** names is equivalent to signatures; those who patronized moneylenders were required to sign a book as record of the debt.

24. **compliment:** the exchange of polite formality.

25. **dog-apes:** dog-faced baboons. The encounter of two such animals would provoke sounds which resembled gibberish to human ears.

26-7. **I have given him a penny, and he renders me the beggarly thanks:** probably the meaning is that the man who gives him extravagant thanks for a slight favor reminds him of a beggar who is cringingly grateful for a pittance because he feels it is expected of him.

29. **cover:** lay the table.

31. **look:** look for.

A dog-faced baboon.
From Konrad Gesner, *Historiae animalium* (1585)

   Unto the sweet bird's throat,
  Come hither, come hither, come hither!   5
    Here shall he see
    No enemy
  But winter and rough weather.

Jaq. More, more, I prithee more!

Ami. It will make you melancholy, Monsieur Jaques.   10

Jaq. I thank it. More, I prithee more! I can suck melancholy out of a song as a weasel sucks eggs. More, I prithee more!

Ami. My voice is ragged. I know I cannot please you.   15

Jaq. I do not desire you to please me; I do desire you to sing. Come, more! another stanzo! Call you 'em stanzos?

Ami. What you will, Monsieur Jaques.

Jaq. Nay, I care not for their names; they owe me 20 nothing. Will you sing?

Ami. More at your request than to please myself.

Jaq. Well then, if ever I thank any man, I'll thank you. But that they call compliment is like the encounter of two dog-apes; and when a man thanks me 25 heartily, methinks I have given him a penny, and he renders me the beggarly thanks. Come, sing! and you that will not, hold your tongues.

Ami. Well, I'll end the song. Sirs, cover the while; the Duke will drink under this tree. He hath been all 30 this day to look you.

Jaq. And I have been all this day to avoid him. He is too disputable for my company. I think of as many

44. **note:** tune.

45. **in despite of my invention:** by taxing my imagination to its utmost.

51. **stubborn:** perverse; see I. i. 135-36 and II. i. 20.

52. **Ducdame:** possibly a fossilized refrain of an old song.

54. **Gross:** glaringly evident, great.

55. **An if:** if.

matters as he; but I give heaven thanks and make no
boast of them. Come, warble, come.   35

Song.

All together here.

>   Who doth ambition shun
>   And loves to live i' the sun,
>   Seeking the food he eats,
>   And pleased with what he gets,
>   Come hither, come hither, come hither!   40
>   Here shall he see
>   No enemy
>   But winter and rough weather.

Jaq. I'll give you a verse to this note that I made
yesterday in despite of my invention.   45
Ami. And I'll sing it.
Jaq. Thus it goes:

>   If it do come to pass
>   That any man turn ass,
>   Leaving his wealth and ease   50
>   A stubborn will to please,
>   Ducdame, ducdame, ducdame!
>   Here shall he see
>   Gross fools as he,
>   An if he will come to me.   55

Ami. What's that "ducdame"?

57-8. **circle:** i.e., such a circle as a magician might draw to summon a demon.

59. **the first-born of Egypt:** all great men, the Duke in particular, since their fates decide those of lesser men. The reference is to the destruction of the first-born of Egypt which forced the Israelites to exchange the settled life of Egypt for a period of wandering.

II. vi. Adam and Orlando appear in the Forest of Arden. Lack of food and the exertion of their journey have exhausted Adam, and Orlando leaves him to rest while he searches for food.

---

8. **Thy conceit is nearer death than thy powers:** conceit means "imagination"; in other words, Adam only thinks his strength is exhausted completely.

9. **be comfortable:** take comfort.

13. **said:** done. Orlando sees some sign of rallying in the old man.

Jaq. 'Tis a Greek invocation to call fools into a circle. I'll go sleep, if I can; if I cannot, I'll rail against all the first-born of Egypt.

Ami. And I'll go seek the Duke. His banquet is prepared. 60

> *Exeunt [severally].*

Scene VI. [The Forest.]

Enter *Orlando* and *Adam.*

Adam. Dear master, I can go no further. O, I die for food! Here lie I down and measure out my grave. Farewell, kind master.

Orl. Why, how now, Adam? no greater heart in thee? Live a little, comfort a little, cheer thyself a 5 little. If this uncouth forest yield anything savage, I will either be food for it or bring it for food to thee. Thy conceit is nearer death than thy powers. For my sake be comfortable; hold death awhile at the arm's end. I will here be with thee presently; and if I bring 10 thee not something to eat, I will give thee leave to die; but if thou diest before I come, thou art a mocker of my labor. Well said! thou lookst cheerly, and I'll be with thee quickly. Yet thou liest in the bleak air. Come, I will bear thee to some shelter, and thou shalt 15 not die for lack of a dinner if there live anything in this desert. Cheerly, good Adam!

> *Exeunt.*

II. vii. Duke Senior is baiting Jaques when Orlando enters and demands food for himself and Adam. The Duke greets him with courtesy and he and Adam are freely offered a share in the banquet.

⸻

5. **compact of jars:** full of discord.

6. **discord in the spheres:** discordancies in place of the heavenly music that the spheres were supposed to make in their revolution, though only angels could hear it.

14. **motley:** i.e., dressed in the characteristic multicolored clothes of a court jester.

18. **good set:** well-phrased.

21. **dial:** perhaps a watch, though a portable sundial may be meant; **poke:** pouch or purse.

From Desiderius Erasmus, *Morias enkomion* (1676).

Scene VII. [The Forest.]

Enter Duke Senior, [Amiens,] and Lords, like
Outlaws.

Duke S. I think he be transformed into a beast,
For I can nowhere find him like a man.
1. Lord. My lord, he is but even now gone hence.
Here was he merry, hearing of a song.
Duke S. If he, compact of jars, grow musical,   5
We shall have shortly discord in the spheres.
Go seek him; tell him I would speak with him.

Enter *Jaques.*

1. Lord. He saves my labor by his own approach.
Duke S. Why, how now, monsieur! what a life is
    this,   10
That your poor friends must woo your company!
What, you look merrily.
Jaq. A fool, a fool! I met a fool i' the forest,
A motley fool!—a miserable world!—
As I do live by food, I met a fool,   15
Who laid him down and basked him in the sun
And railed on Lady Fortune in good terms,
In good set terms—and yet a motley fool.
"Good morrow, fool," quoth I. "No, sir," quoth he,
"Call me not fool till heaven hath sent me fortune."   20
And then he drew a dial from his poke,
And looking on it with lackluster eye,
Says very wisely, "It is ten o'clock.

31. chanticleer: the name of the cock in the folk tale of *Reynard the Fox*.

33. sans: without.

42. vents: gives out.

47-9. weed your better judgments/ Of all opinion that grows rank in them/ That I am wise: eliminate your opinion that I am wise and give me license to speak freely as a fool.

52. galled: rubbed raw.

Fools hunting.
From Desiderius Erasmus, *Morias enkomion* (1676).

Thus we may see," quoth he, "how the world wags.
'Tis but an hour ago since it was nine,   25
And after one hour more 'twill be eleven;
And so, from hour to hour, we ripe and ripe,
And then, from hour to hour, we rot and rot;
And thereby hangs a tale." When I did hear
The motley fool thus moral on the time,   30
My lungs began to crow like chanticleer
That fools should be so deep contemplative;
And I did laugh sans intermission
An hour by his dial. O noble fool!
A worthy fool! Motley's the only wear!   35
   Duke S. What fool is this?
   Jaq. O worthy fool! One that hath been a courtier,
And says, if ladies be but young and fair,
They have the gift to know it. And in his brain,
Which is as dry as the remainder biscuit   40
After a voyage, he hath strange places crammed
With observation, the which he vents
In mangled forms. O that I were a fool!
I am ambitious for a motley coat.
   Duke S. Thou shalt have one.   45
   Jaq.   It is my only suit,
Provided that you weed your better judgments
Of all opinion that grows rank in them
That I am wise. I must have liberty
Withal, as large a charter as the wind,   50
To blow on whom I please; for so fools have.
And they that are most galled with my folly,
They most must laugh. And why, sir, must they so?
The why is plain as way to parish church:

55-7. **He that a fool doth very wisely hit/ Doth very foolishly, although he smart,/ Not to seem senseless of the bob:** the butt of a fool's jest is foolish to show his hurt. **Bob** means bitter jest.

58. **anatomized:** dissected; see I. i. 148.

59. **squandering glances:** chance hits.

60. **Invest:** clothe.

66. **counter:** a small token or coin of little value. Jaques ironically challenges the Duke to explain himself.

69. **brutish sting:** carnal impulse.

70. **embossed:** swollen.

73. **pride:** ostentatious dress.

74. **tax:** blame; see I. ii. 82.

82. **function:** occupation.

83. **bravery:** splendid clothes; **is not on my cost:** costs me nothing.

84-5. **suits/ His folly to the mettle of my speech:** displays the very folly I have described.

He that a fool doth very wisely hit   55
Doth very foolishly, although he smart,
Not to seem senseless of the bob. If not,
The wise man's folly is anatomized
Even by the squandering glances of the fool.
Invest me in my motley. Give me leave   60
To speak my mind, and I will through and through
Cleanse the foul body of the infected world,
If they will patiently receive my medicine.
    Duke S. Fie on thee! I can tell what thou wouldst
      do.   65
    Jaq. What, for a counter, would I do but good?
    Duke S. Most mischievous foul sin, in chiding sin.
For thou thyself hast been a libertine,
As sensual as the brutish sting itself;
And all the embossed sores and headed evils   70
That thou with license of free foot hast caught,
Wouldst thou disgorge into the general world.
    Jaq. Why, who cries out on pride
That can therein tax any private party?
Doth it not flow as hugely as the sea   75
Till that the wearer's very means do ebb?
What woman in the city do I name
When that I say the city woman bears
The cost of princes on unworthy shoulders?
Who can come in and say that I mean her,   80
When such a one as she, such is her neighbor?
Or what is he of basest function
That says his bravery is not on my cost,
Thinking that I mean him, but therein suits
His folly to the mettle of my speech?   85

87. **do him right:** portray him correctly.

88. **free:** innocent.

100. **touched my vein at first:** hit upon my condition with your first comment.

102. **inland bred:** brought up in a civilized area, not in the rude upland country.

103. **nurture:** cultivation, good manners.

106. **And:** if; **reason:** Jaques is punning on **reason,** a contemporary spelling for "raisin." Apparently raisins were one of the items in the Duke's sparse fare.

A good man's feast.
From Francis Thynne (?), *A Book of Divers Devices*
(1593-1622).

There then! how then? what then? Let me see wherein
My tongue hath wronged him. If it do him right,
Then he hath wronged himself. If he be free,
Why, then my taxing like a wild goose flies,
Unclaimed of any man. But who comes here? 90

Enter *Orlando*.

Orl. Forbear, and eat no more!
Jaq.   Why, I have eat
    none yet.
Orl. Nor shalt not, till necessity be served.
Jaq. Of what kind should this cock come of? 95
Duke S. Art thou thus boldened, man, by thy dis-
    tress,
Or else a rude despiser of good manners,
That in civility thou seemst so empty?
Orl. You touched my vein at first. The thorny point 100
Of bare distress hath ta'en from me the show
Of smooth civility; yet am I inland bred
And know some nurture. But forbear, I say!
He dies that touches any of this fruit
Till I and my affairs are answered. 105
Jaq. And you will not be answered with reason, I
must die.
Duke S. What would you have? Your gentleness
    shall force
More than your force move us to gentleness. 110
Orl. I almost die for food, and let me have it!
Duke S. Sit down and feed, and welcome to our
    table.

116. **countenance:** general behavior, not "face"; see I. i. 17.
122. **knolled:** rung.
133. **upon command:** for the asking.
139. **sufficed:** satisfied.
140. **weak:** that is, weakening.
143. **waste:** use up; see II. iv. 98.

Orl. Speak you so gently? Pardon me, I pray you.
I thought that all things had been savage here,   115
And therefore put I on the countenance
Of stern commandment. But whate'er you are
That in this desert inaccessible,
Under the shade of melancholy boughs,
Lose and neglect the creeping hours of time—   120
If ever you have looked on better days,
If ever been where bells have knolled to church,
If ever sat at any good man's feast,
If ever from your eyelids wiped a tear
And know what 'tis to pity and be pitied,   125
Let gentleness my strong enforcement be;
In the which hope I blush, and hide my sword.

Duke S. True is it that we have seen better days,
And have with holy bell been knolled to church,
And sat at good men's feasts, and wiped our eyes   130
Of drops that sacred pity hath engendered;
And therefore sit you down in gentleness,
And take upon command what help we have
That to your wanting may be ministered.

Orl. Then but forbear your food a little while,   135
Whiles, like a doe, I go to find my fawn
And give it food. There is an old poor man
Who after me hath many a weary step
Limped in pure love. Till he be first sufficed,
Oppressed with two weak evils, age and hunger,   140
I will not touch a bit.

Duke S.   Go find him out,
And we will nothing waste till you return.

154. **Mewling:** crying feebly.

160. **pard:** panther.

161. **Jealous in honor:** i.e., jealous (touchy) about his honor.

166. **saws:** sayings, maxims; **modern instances:** commonplace as proofs of his wisdom. **Modern** means "ordinary."

168. **pantaloon:** a character from the Italian *commedia dell' arte:* a foolish old man.

170. **youthful hose:** i.e., the breeches he had when young.

173. **his:** its.

A pantaloon.
From Desiderius Erasmus, *Morias enkomion* (1676).

Orl. I thank ye, and be blest for your good comfort!
[*Exit.*]

Duke S. Thou seest we are not all alone unhappy. 145
This wide and universal theatre
Presents more woeful pageants than the scene
Wherein we play in.

Jaq.   All the world's a stage,
And all the men and women merely players.   150
They have their exits and their entrances,
And one man in his time plays many parts,
His acts being seven ages. At first, the infant,
Mewling and puking in the nurse's arms.
Then the whining schoolboy, with his satchel   155
And shining morning face, creeping like snail
Unwillingly to school. And then the lover,
Sighing like furnace, with a woeful ballad
Made to his mistress' eyebrow. Then a soldier,
Full of strange oaths and bearded like the pard,   160
Jealous in honor, sudden and quick in quarrel,
Seeking the bubble reputation
Even in the cannon's mouth. And then the justice,
In fair round belly with good capon lined,
With eyes severe and beard of formal cut,   165
Full of wise saws and modern instances;
And so he plays his part. The sixth age shifts
Into the lean and slippered pantaloon,
With spectacles on nose and pouch on side;
His youthful hose, well saved, a world too wide   170
For his shrunk shank, and his big manly voice,
Turning again toward childish treble, pipes
And whistles in his sound. Last scene of all,

The babe "mewling and puking" in the nurse's arms.
From Desiderius Erasmus, *Moriæ enkomion* (1676).

192. feigning: pretense.

That ends this strange eventful history,
Is second childishness and mere oblivion,   175
Sans teeth, sans eyes, sans taste, sans everything.

Enter *Orlando*, with *Adam*.

Duke S. Welcome. Set down your venerable burden
And let him feed.
Orl. I thank you most for him.
Adam.   So had you need.   180
I scarce can speak to thank you for myself.
Duke S. Welcome, fall to. I will not trouble you
As yet to question you about your fortunes.
Give us some music; and, good cousin, sing.

Song.

Ami. Blow, blow, thou winter wind,   185
   Thou art not so unkind
     As man's ingratitude.
   Thy tooth is not so keen,
   Because thou art not seen,
     Although thy breath be rude.   190
Heigh-ho, sing heigh-ho, unto the green holly!
Most friendship is feigning, most loving mere
        folly:
   Then, heigh-ho, the holly!
   This life is most jolly.   195

   Freeze, freeze, thou bitter sky,
   That dost not bite so nigh

206. **effigies:** likenesses.
207. **limned:** pictured.
209. **residue of your fortune:** rest of your story.

As benefits forgot.
Though thou the waters warp,
Thy sting is not so sharp　　　　　　　　　200
As friend remembered not.
Heigh-ho! sing, &c.

Duke S. If that you were the good Sir Rowland's
son—
As you have whispered faithfully you were,　　205
And as mine eye doth his effigies witness
Most truly limned and living in your face—
Be truly welcome hither. I am the Duke
That loved your father. The residue of your fortune,
Go to my cave and tell me. Good old man,　　210
Thou art right welcome, as thy master is.
Support him by the arm. Give me your hand,
And let me all your fortunes understand.

　　　　　　　　　　　　　　Exeunt.

AS YOU LIKE IT

ACT III

III. i. Oliver is haled before Duke Frederick, who orders the seizure of all his worldly goods until he produces Orlando to tell what he knows of the runaways.

▬▬▬▬▬▬▬▬▬▬

2. the better part made mercy: composed more of mercy than revenge.

3. absent argument: i.e., Orlando. He means he would wreak his revenge on Oliver and not waste time on Orlando.

6. Seek him with candle: search every dark corner.

11. quit: acquit.

17. officers of such a nature: appropriate officials.

18. Make an extent upon: legal terminology meaning to seize by writ of extent.

19. expediently: speedily.

ACT III

Scene I. [A room in the Palace.]

Enter *Duke* [*Frederick*], *Lords,* and *Oliver.*

Duke. Not see him since? Sir, sir, that cannot be!
But were I not the better part made mercy,
I should not seek an absent argument
Of my revenge, thou present. But look to it!
Find out thy brother, wheresoe'er he is;   5
Seek him with candle; bring him dead or living
Within this twelvemonth, or turn thou no more
To seek a living in our territory.
Thy lands, and all things that thou dost call thine
Worth seizure, do we seize into our hands   10
Till thou canst quit thee by thy brother's mouth
Of what we think against thee.

Oli. O that your Highness knew my heart in this!
I never loved my brother in my life.

Duke. More villain thou! Well, push him out of   15
    doors,
And let my officers of such a nature
Make an extent upon his house and lands.
Do this expediently and turn him going.

Exeunt.

45

III. ii. Orlando decorates the forest with verses on Rosalind's beauty. Celia and Rosalind find some of the verses and Celia reveals that Orlando is the poet. When Orlando himself appears, Rosalind, confident in her disguise, jests with him about his foolish love, and offers to cure him by posing as his mistress to demonstrate the fickleness of feminine behavior.

━━━━━━━━━━━━━━━━━━

2. **thrice-crowned Queen of Night:** the moon goddess Diana.

4. **Thy huntress' name:** one of Diana's followers, meaning a virgin; **sway:** rule.

6. **character:** write out.

8. **witnessed:** evidenced.

10. **unexpressive:** indescribable.

16. **private:** secluded.

19. **spare:** austere; **humor:** disposition.

Scene II. [The Forest.]

Enter Orlando, [hanging a paper on a tree].

Orl. Hang there, my verse, in witness of my love;
   And thou, thrice-crowned Queen of Night, survey
With thy chaste eye, from thy pale sphere above,
   Thy huntress' name that my full life doth sway.
O Rosalind! these trees shall be my books,   5
   And in their barks my thoughts I'll character,
That every eye which in this forest looks
   Shall see thy virtue witnessed everywhere.
Run, run, Orlando! carve on every tree
The fair, the chaste, and unexpressive she.   *Exit.* 10

Enter Corin and [Touchstone the] Clown.

Cor. And how like you this shepherd's life, Master
Touchstone?
Touch. Truly, shepherd, in respect of itself, it is a
good life; but in respect that it is a shepherd's life,
it is naught. In respect that it is solitary, I like it very   15
well; but in respect that it is private, it is a very vile
life. Now in respect it is in the fields, it pleaseth me
well; but in respect it is not in the court, it is tedious.
As it is a spare life, look you, it fits my humor well;
but as there is no more plenty in it, it goes much   20
against my stomach. Hast any philosophy in thee,
shepherd?
Cor. No more but that I know the more one

29-31. **he that hath learned no wit by nature nor art may complain of good breeding, or comes of a very dull kindred:** he that has no knowledge by inheritance or industry is likely to complain of his lack of education unless he is very dull indeed.

44. **parlous:** perilous.

52. **still:** always; see I. ii. 223, I. iii. 77.

53. **fells:** pelts.

A courtier and a country bumpkin.
From Robert Greene, *A Quip for an Upstart Courtier: or, A Quaint Dispute between Velvet Breeches and Cloth Breeches* (1592).

sickens, the worse at ease he is; and that he that
wants money, means, and content is without three   25
good friends; that the property of rain is to wet and
fire to burn; that good pasture makes fat sheep, and
that a great cause of the night is lack of the sun; that
he that hath learned no wit by nature nor art may
complain of good breeding, or comes of a very dull   30
kindred.

Touch. Such a one is a natural philosopher. Wast
ever in court, shepherd?

Cor. No, truly.

Touch. Then thou art damned.   35

Cor. Nay, I hope.

Touch. Truly thou art damned, like an ill-roasted
egg, all on one side.

Cor. For not being at court! Your reason.

Touch. Why, if thou never wast at court, thou   40
never sawst good manners; if thou never sawst good
manners, then thy manners must be wicked; and
wickedness is sin, and sin is damnation. Thou art in a
parlous state, shepherd.

Cor. Not a whit, Touchstone. Those that are good   45
manners at the court are as ridiculous in the country
as the behavior of the country is most mockable at
the court. You told me you salute not at the court
but you kiss your hands. That courtesy would be uncleanly if courtiers were shepherds.   50

Touch. Instance, briefly. Come, instance.

Cor. Why, we are still handling our ewes, and their
fells you know are greasy.

Touch. Why, do not your courtier's hands sweat?

63. **civet:** perfume derived from the musk of a civet cat.

64-5. **in respect of:** in comparison with.

66. **perpend:** consider.

67. **Mend the instance:** give a better example.

71. **God make incision in thee:** God help thee by surgery; **raw:** uncouth.

74-5. **content with my harm:** reconciled to the misfortunes which beset me.

80. **bell-wether:** bell-wearing leader of a flock.

81. **cuckoldly ram:** a cuckold, that is a man betrayed by his wife, was said by the Elizabethans to wear horns.

Shearing sheep.
From Pietro de Crescenzi, *Nel quale si trattano gli ordini di tutte le cose che si appartengono a commodi e a gli utili della villa* (1561).

and is not the grease of a mutton as wholesome as the 55
sweat of a man? Shallow, shallow! A better instance,
I say. Come.

Cor. Besides, our hands are hard.

Touch. Your lips will feel them the sooner. Shallow
again! A more sounder instance, come. 60

Cor. And they are often tarred over with the surgery of our sheep, and would you have us kiss tar?
The courtier's hands are perfumed with civet.

Touch. Most shallow man! Thou worm's meat in
respect of a good piece of flesh indeed! Learn of the 65
wise, and perpend. Civet is of a baser birth than tar—
the very uncleanly flux of a cat. Mend the instance,
shepherd.

Cor. You have too courtly a wit for me. I'll rest.

Touch. Wilt thou rest damned? God help thee, 70
shallow man! God make incision in thee, thou art raw!

Cor. Sir, I am a true laborer: I earn that I eat, get
that I wear; owe no man hate, envy no man's happiness; glad of other men's good, content with my
harm; and the greatest of my pride is to see my ewes 75
graze and my lambs suck.

Touch. That is another simple sin in you: to bring
the ewes and the rams together and to offer to get
your living by the copulation of cattle; to be bawd to
a bell-wether, and to betray a she-lamb of a twelve- 80
month to a crooked-pated old cuckoldly ram, out of
all reasonable match. If thou beest not damned for
this, the devil himself will have no shepherds; I cannot see else how thou shouldst scape.

87. **western Ind:** the West Indies.

91. **lined:** portrayed.

97. **the right butterwomen's rank to market:** Touchstone suggests that the jog-trot verse is like the pace of butterwomen's horses ambling to market.

100. **hart:** male red deer; **hind:** female red deer.

Cor. Here comes young Master Ganymede, my new   85
mistress's brother.

Enter *Rosalind,* [reading a paper].

Ros. "From the east to western Ind,
        No jewel is like Rosalind.
        Her worth, being mounted on the wind,
        Through all the world bears Rosalind.   90
        All the pictures fairest lined
        Are but black to Rosalind.
        Let no face be kept in mind
        But the fair of Rosalind."

Touch. I'll rhyme you so eight years together, din-   95
ners and suppers and sleeping hours excepted. It is
the right butterwomen's rank to market.
Ros. Out, fool!
Touch. For a taste:

        If a hart do lack a hind,   100
        Let him seek out Rosalind.
        If the cat will after kind,
        So be sure will Rosalind.
        Winter garments must be lined,
        So must slender Rosalind.   105
        They that reap must sheaf and bind,
        Then to cart with Rosalind.
        Sweetest nut hath sourest rind,
        Such a nut is Rosalind.

117. **medlar:** small fruit between an apple and a pear, eaten only when so ripe that it is nearly rotten.

He that sweetest rose will find   110
Must find love's prick, and Rosalind.

This is the very false gallop of verses! Why do you
infect yourself with them?

Ros. Peace, you dull fool! I found them on a tree.

Touch. Truly the tree yields bad fruit.   115

Ros. I'll graff it with you and then I shall graff it
with a medlar. Then it will be the earliest fruit i' the
country; for you'll be rotten ere you be half ripe, and
that's the right virtue of the medlar.

Touch. You have said; but whether wisely or no, 120
let the forest judge.

Enter *Celia*, with a writing.

Ros. Peace!
Here comes my sister reading. Stand aside.

Cel. "Why should this a desert be,
     For it is unpeopled? No!   125
   Tongues I'll hang on every tree
     That shall civil sayings show:
   Some, how brief the life of man
     Runs his erring pilgrimage,
   That the stretching of a span   130
     Buckles in his sum of age;
   Some, of violated vows
     'Twixt the souls of friend and friend;
   But upon the fairest boughs,

138-39. The quintessence of every sprite/ Heaven would in little show: Heaven would reveal in miniature the essence of every individual.

142. wide-enlarged: amply demonstrated.

144. not her heart: i.e., because she was faithless.

146. Atalanta's better part: Atalanta in Greek mythology was a virgin huntress also famous for her physical beauty and speed in running. Suitors who could not outrun her were put to death.

147. Lucretia: a chaste Roman matron who killed herself for shame after her rape by Tarquin. Shakespeare expanded the theme in one of his narrative poems.

149. synod: council.

151. touches: characteristics.

154. pulpiter: correction by James Spedding for the Folio reading "Jupiter."

161. scrip: an archaic word for a kind of bag carried by wayfarers.

Or at every sentence end,   135
Will I 'Rosalinda' write,
  Teaching all that read to know
The quintessence of every sprite
  Heaven would in little show.
Therefore heaven Nature charged   140
  That one body should be filled
With all graces wide-enlarged.
  Nature presently distilled
Helen's cheek, but not her heart,
  Cleopatra's majesty,   145
Atalanta's better part,
  Sad Lucretia's modesty.
Thus Rosalind of many parts
  By heavenly synod was devised,
Of many faces, eyes, and hearts,   150
  To have the touches dearest prized.
Heaven would that she these gifts should have,
And I to live and die her slave."

Ros. O most gentle pulpiter! what tedious homily
of love have you wearied your parishioners withal, 155
and never cried, "Have patience, good people"!

Cel. How now? Back, friends. Shepherd, go off a
little. Go with him, sirrah.

Touch. Come, shepherd, let us make an honorable
retreat; though not with bag and baggage, yet with 160
scrip and scrippage. *Exeunt* [*Corin and Touchstone*].

Cel. Didst thou hear these verses?

Ros. O, yes, I heard them all, and more too; for

174-75. **seven of the nine days out of the wonder:** a "nine days' wonder" was a proverbial phrase of ancient lineage indicating that no wonder seemed wondrous for more than nine days.

176-77. **Pythagoras' time:** a reference to the Pythagorean theory of the transmigration of souls. The soul of a human might come to rest in a rat. The allusion to rhyming refers to spells said to destroy rats.

179. **Trow you who:** whom do you believe.

184-86. **it is a hard matter for friends to meet; but mountains may be removed with earthquakes, and so encounter:** an inversion of a proverb: "Friends may meet, but mountains never greet."

193. **hooping:** whooping; that is, beyond all wonder.

194. **Good my complexion:** a mild expletive, equivalent to "God help my disposition."

some of them had in them more feet than the verses
would bear.   165

Cel. That's no matter. The feet might bear the
verses.

Ros. Ay, but the feet were lame, and could not
bear themselves without the verse, and therefore
stood lamely in the verse.   170

Cel. But didst thou hear without wondering how
thy name should be hanged and carved upon these
trees?

Ros. I was seven of the nine days out of the wonder before you came; for look here what I found on a 175
palm tree. I was never so berhymed since Pythagoras'
time that I was an Irish rat, which I can hardly remember.

Cel. Trow you who hath done this?

Ros. Is it a man?   180

Cel. And a chain that you once wore, about his
neck. Change you color?

Ros. I prithee who?

Cel. O Lord, Lord! it is a hard matter for friends to
meet; but mountains may be removed with earth- 185
quakes, and so encounter.

Ros. Nay, but who is it?

Cel. Is it possible?

Ros. Nay, I prithee now with most petitionary
vehemence, tell me who it is.   190

Cel. O wonderful, wonderful, and most wonderful
wonderful! and yet again wonderful, and after that,
out of all hooping!

Ros. Good my complexion! Dost thou think, though

195. **caparisoned:** outfitted, dressed.

196-97. **a South Sea of discovery:** i.e., equivalent to the long period of time needed to explore the South Seas.

198. **apace:** with despatch, quickly.

205. **of God's making:** a proper, well-formed man.

209. **stay:** wait for; see I. i. 7.

213-14. **sad brow and true maid:** gravely and sincerely. **Sad** is used in the sense of "serious" rather than unhappy.

220. **Wherein:** i.e., in what garb.

224. **Gargantua's mouth:** the mouth of a giant. **Gargantua,** besides appearing in Rabelais's *Gargantua and Pantagruel,* was known in England from tales by other writers.

I am caparisoned like a man, I have a doublet and 195
hose in my disposition? One inch of delay more is a
South Sea of discovery. I prithee tell me who is it
quickly, and speak apace. I would thou couldst stam-
mer, that thou mightst pour this concealed man out of
thy mouth as wine comes out of a narrow-mouthed 200
bottle—either too much at once, or none at all. I
prithee take the cork out of thy mouth, that I may
drink thy tidings.

Cel. So you may put a man in your belly.

Ros. Is he of God's making? What manner of man? 205
Is his head worth a hat? or his chin worth a beard?

Cel. Nay, he hath but a little beard.

Ros. Why, God will send more, if the man will be
thankful! Let me stay the growth of his beard, if thou
delay me not the knowledge of his chin.   210

Cel. It is young Orlando, that tripped up the
wrestler's heels and your heart both in an instant.

Ros. Nay, but the devil take mocking! Speak sad
brow and true maid.

Cel. I' faith, coz, 'tis he.   215

Ros. Orlando?

Cel. Orlando.

Ros. Alas the day! what shall I do with my doublet
and hose? What did he when thou sawst him? What
said he? How looked he? Wherein went he? What 220
makes he here? Did he ask for me? Where remains
he? How parted he with thee? and when shalt thou
see him again? Answer me in one word.

Cel. You must borrow me Gargantua's mouth first;
'tis a word too great for any mouth of this age's size. 225

229. **Looks he as freshly:** is he still as good looking.

231. **resolve:** satisfy, answer.

232. **propositions:** questions.

233. **observance:** attention.

237. **Give me audience:** hear me; let me go on.

243. **"holla":** whoa.

243-44 **curvets unseasonably:** frolics inappropriately, like a horse feeling his oats; **furnished:** dressed and equipped.

245. **heart:** a pun on "heart/hart."

246. **burden:** a subordinate refrain accompanying a song.

250. **bring me out:** put me off, see l. 247; **Soft:** hold.

252. **good faith:** truly.

To say ay and no to these particulars is more than to
answer in a catechism.

Ros. But doth he know that I am in this forest, and
in man's apparel? Looks he as freshly as he did the
day he wrestled?   230

Cel. It is as easy to count atomies as to resolve the
propositions of a lover; but take a taste of my finding
him, and relish it with good observance. I found him
under a tree, like a dropped acorn.

Ros. It may well be called Jove's tree when it drops 235
forth such fruit.

Cel. Give me audience, good madam.

Ros. Proceed.

Cel. There lay he stretched along like a wounded
knight.   240

Ros. Though it be pity to see such a sight, it well
becomes the ground.

Cel. Cry "holla" to thy tongue, I prithee. It curvets
unseasonably. He was furnished like a hunter.

Ros. O, ominous! he comes to kill my heart.   245

Cel. I would sing my song without a burden. Thou
bringst me out of tune.

Ros. Do you not know I am a woman? When I
think, I must speak. Sweet, say on.

Enter *Orlando* and *Jaques.*

Cel. You bring me out. Soft! comes he not here?   250

Ros. 'Tis he; slink by and note him.

Jaq. I thank you for your company; but, good faith,
I had as lief have been myself alone.

Atalanta racing.
From Gabriel Simeoni, *La vita et Metamorfoseo d'Ovidio* (1559).

254. **fashion sake:** fashion's sake; that is, courtesy.

260. **mo:** more.

261. **ill-favoredly:** ungraciously.

270. **conned:** learned.

271. **rings:** posy rings, so called because of the rhymes inscribed on them.

272. **right painted cloth:** exactly like hangings on which were painted pictures and maxims, sometimes in question and answer form.

Orl. And so had I; but yet for fashion sake I thank
you too for your society.   255

Jaq. God be wi' you! Let's meet as little as we can.

Orl. I do desire we may be better strangers.

Jaq. I pray you mar no more trees with writing
love songs in their barks.

Orl. I pray you mar no mo of my verses with read-   260
ing them ill-favoredly.

Jaq. Rosalind is your love's name?

Orl. Yes, just.

Jaq. I do not like her name.

Orl. There was no thought of pleasing you when   265
she was christened.

Jaq. What stature is she of?

Orl. Just as high as my heart.

Jaq. You are full of pretty answers. Have you not
been acquainted with goldsmiths' wives, and conned   270
them out of rings?

Orl. Not so; but I answer you right painted cloth,
from whence you have studied your questions.

Jaq. You have a nimble wit; I think 'twas made of
Atalanta's heels. Will you sit down with me? and we   275
two will rail against our mistress the world and all our
misery.

Orl. I will chide no breather in the world but myself, against whom I know most faults.

Jaq. The worst fault you have is to be in love.   280

Orl. 'Tis a fault I will not change for your best virtue. I am weary of you.

Jaq. By my troth, I was seeking for a fool when I
found you.

288. **cipher:** zero; a nonentity.

294. **lackey:** servant; **under that habit:** in that garb.

302. **detect:** reveal.

305. **divers:** various, different.

312. **se'nnight:** seven nights, a week.

Orl. He is drowned in the brook. Look but in and 285
you shall see him.

Jaq. There I shall see mine own figure.

Orl. Which I take to be either a fool or a cipher.

Jaq. I'll tarry no longer with you. Farewell, good
Signior Love.   290

Orl. I am glad of your departure. Adieu, good
Monsieur Melancholy.

[*Exit Jaques.*]

Ros. [*Aside to Celia*] I will speak to him like a
saucy lackey, and under that habit play the knave
with him.—Do you hear, forester?   295

Orl. Very well. What would you?

Ros. I pray you, what is't o'clock?

Orl. You should ask me, what time o' day. There's
no clock in the forest.

Ros. Then there is no true lover in the forest; else 300
sighing every minute and groaning every hour would
detect the lazy foot of Time as well as a clock.

Orl. And why not the swift foot of Time? Had not
that been as proper?

Ros. By no means, sir. Time travels in divers paces 305
with divers persons. I'll tell you who Time ambles
withal, who Time trots withal, who Time gallops
withal, and who he stands still withal.

Orl. I prithee, who doth he trot withal?

Ros. Marry, he trots hard with a young maid be- 310
tween the contract of her marriage and the day it is
solemnized. If the interim be but a se'nnight, Time's
pace is so hard that it seems the length of seven year.

319. **wasteful:** wasting, exhausting.

324. **softly:** slowly.

334. **cony:** rabbit.

335. **kindled:** littered, born. Used in this sense mainly of rabbits.

336. **something:** somewhat; see II. iv. 59.

337. **purchase:** acquire.

338. **of:** by.

343. **touched:** marred.

343-44. **giddy offenses:** capricious faults.

Orl. Who ambles Time withal?

Ros. With a priest that lacks Latin and a rich man 315
that hath not the gout; for the one sleeps easily because he cannot study, and the other lives merrily because he feels no pain; the one lacking the burden of
lean and wasteful learning, the other knowing no burden of heavy tedious penury. These Time ambles 320
withal.

Orl. Who doth he gallop withal?

Ros. With a thief to the gallows; for though he go
as softly as foot can fall, he thinks himself too soon
there. 325

Orl. Who stays it still withal?

Ros. With lawyers in the vacation; for they sleep
between term and term, and then they perceive not
how time moves.

Orl. Where dwell you, pretty youth? 330

Ros. With this shepherdess, my sister; here in the
skirts of the forest, like fringe upon a petticoat.

Orl. Are you native of this place?

Ros. As the cony that you see dwell where she is
kindled. 335

Orl. Your accent is something finer than you could
purchase in so removed a dwelling.

Ros. I have been told so of many. But indeed an old
religious uncle of mine taught me to speak, who was
in his youth an inland man; one that knew courtship 340
too well, for there he fell in love. I have heard him
read many lectures against it; and I thank God I am
not a woman, to be touched with so many giddy

352. **physic:** medicine; see I. i. 83.

357. **fancy-monger:** dealer in love.

359. **quotidian:** a fever of daily occurrence, said to be a symptom of love.

364. **cage of rushes:** an ineffectual prison for anyone wishing to be free.

366. **blue:** that is, blue-shadowed from sleeplessness.

367. **unquestionable:** untalkative; having no taste for conversation.

370. **your having in beard is a younger brother's revenue:** your possession of beard is slight, like the inheritance of a younger brother.

371-72. **bonnet unbanded:** hat unornamented.

offenses as he hath generally taxed their whole sex withal. 345

Orl. Can you remember any of the principal evils that he laid to the charge of women?

Ros. There were none principal. They were all like one another as halfpence are, every one fault seeming monstrous till his fellow-fault came to match it. 350

Orl. I prithee recount some of them.

Ros. No, I will not cast away my physic but on those that are sick. There is a man haunts the forest that abuses our young plants with carving "Rosalind" on their barks; hangs odes upon hawthorns, and 355 elegies on brambles; all, forsooth, deifying the name of Rosalind. If I could meet that fancy-monger, I would give him some good counsel, for he seems to have the quotidian of love upon him.

Orl. I am he that is so love-shaked. I pray you tell 360 me your remedy.

Ros. There is none of my uncle's marks upon you. He taught me how to know a man in love; in which cage of rushes I am sure you are not prisoner.

Orl. What were his marks? 365

Ros. A lean cheek, which you have not; a blue eye and sunken, which you have not; an unquestionable spirit, which you have not; a beard neglected, which you have not. But I pardon you for that, for simply your having in beard is a younger brother's revenue. 370 Then your hose should be ungartered, your bonnet unbanded, your sleeve unbuttoned, your shoe untied, and everything about you demonstrating a careless desolation. But you are no such man: you are rather

375. **point-device in your accouterments:** perfectly turned out.

383. **good sooth:** sober truth.

391. **merely:** absolutely; see **mere** II. i. 64.

400. **moonish:** changeable.

401. **liking:** responsive; **fantastical:** fanciful, ruled by whim; see II. iv. 30. **apish:** whimsical.

402-3. **for every passion something and for no passion truly anything:** stirred by every passing mood but incapable of being deeply moved.

405. **color:** kind; see I. ii. 97.

405-6. **entertain:** welcome.

point-device in your accouterments, as loving your- 375
self, than seeming the lover of any other.

Orl. Fair youth, I would I could make thee believe
I love.

Ros. Me believe it? You may as soon make her that
you love believe it, which I warrant she is apter to do 380
than to confess she does. That is one of the points in
the which women still give the lie to their con-
sciences. But in good sooth, are you he that hangs the
verses on the trees wherein Rosalind is so admired?

Orl. I swear to thee, youth, by the white hand of 385
Rosalind, I am that he, that unfortunate he.

Ros. But are you so much in love as your rhymes
speak?

Orl. Neither rhyme nor reason can express how
much. 390

Ros. Love is merely a madness, and, I tell you, deserves as well a dark house and a whip as madmen
do; and the reason why they are not so punished and
cured is that the lunacy is so ordinary that the whip-
pers are in love too. Yet I profess curing it by counsel. 395

Orl. Did you ever cure any so?

Ros. Yes, one, and in this manner. He was to
imagine me his love, his mistress; and I set him every
day to woo me. At which time would I, being but a
moonish youth, grieve, be effeminate, changeable, 400
longing, and liking, proud, fantastical, apish, shallow,
inconstant, full of tears, full of smiles; for every passion something and for no passion truly anything, as
boys and women are for the most part cattle of this
color; would now like him, now loathe him; then en- 405

407. **that:** so that.

407-8. **from his mad humor of love to a living humor of madness:** from his caprice of being in love to actual madness.

410. **merely monastic:** precisely like a monk.

411. **liver:** the source of love in Elizabethan physiology.

419-20. **by the way:** as we go.

—————————————

III. iii. Touchstone has fallen in love with Audrey, a country maid, and considers marrying her—though he would be content with a ceremony that is not too binding.

—————————————

3. **feature:** overall appearance of face and form. Touchstone speaks with mock modesty—and Audrey does not understand him.

4. **warrant:** save.

tertain him, then forswear him; now weep for him,
then spit at him; that I drave my suitor from his mad
humor of love to a living humor of madness, which
was, to forswear the full stream of the world and to
live in a nook merely monastic. And thus I cured him;   410
and this way will I take upon me to wash your liver
as clean as a sound sheep's heart, that there shall not
be one spot of love in't.

Orl. I would not be cured, youth.

Ros. I would cure you, if you would but call me   415
Rosalind and come every day to my cote and woo me.

Orl. Now, by the faith of my love, I will! Tell me
where it is.

Ros. Go with me to it, and I'll show it you; and by
the way you shall tell me where in the forest you live.   420
Will you go?

Orl. With all my heart, good youth.

Ros. Nay, you must call me Rosalind. Come, sister,
will you go?

Exeunt.

Scene III. [The Forest.]

*Enter [Touchstone the] Clown, Audrey; and
Jaques [behind].*

Touch. Come apace, good Audrey. I will fetch up
your goats, Audrey. And how, Audrey, am I the man
yet? Doth my simple feature content you?

Aud. Your features? Lord warrant us! What features!   5

7. **capricious:** a pun on the derivation of the word from the Latin *caper*, goat; **honest:** chaste. Probably said ironically, since Ovid was identified with a flippant attitude towards love.

7-8. **Ovid . . . among the Goths:** Ovid was banished by the Emperor Augustus to live with the Getae, once identified with the Goths.

9. **ill-inhabited:** ill-housed.

10. **Jove in a thatched house:** i.e., when he visited Philemon and Baucis in their modest home (Ovid, *Metamorphoses*, Book 8).

12. **with:** by.

13-4. **it strikes a man more dead than a great reckoning in a little room:** it is more devastating than a large bill for poor accommodations.

19. **feigning:** i.e., creative, imaginative.

21. **feign:** pretend; see II. vii. 192.

25. **honest:** chaste again, as in l. 7.

28. **hard-favored:** unattractive.

31. **material:** full of matter, as the Duke said of Jaques, II. i. 73.

34. **foul:** ugly.

Touch. I am here with thee and thy goats, as the most capricious poet, honest Ovid, was among the Goths.

Jaq. [*Aside*] O knowledge ill-inhabited, worse than Jove in a thatched house! 　　10

Touch. When a man's verses cannot be understood, nor a man's good wit seconded with the forward child, understanding, it strikes a man more dead than a great reckoning in a little room. Truly, I would the gods had made thee poetical. 　　15

Aud. I do not know what poetical is. Is it honest in deed and word? Is it a true thing?

Touch. No, truly; for the truest poetry is the most feigning, and lovers are given to poetry; and what they swear in poetry may be said, as lovers, they do 　20 feign.

Aud. Do you wish then that the gods had made me poetical?

Touch. I do truly. For thou swearest to me thou art honest. Now if thou wert a poet, I might have some 　25 hope thou didst feign.

Aud. Would you not have me honest?

Touch. No, truly, unless thou wert hard-favored; for honesty coupled to beauty is to have honey a sauce to sugar. 　　30

Jaq. [*Aside*] A material fool!

Aud. Well, I am not fair; and therefore I pray the gods make me honest.

Touch. Truly, and to cast away honesty upon a foul slut were to put good meat into an unclean dish. 　35

41. **Martext:** Shakespeare uses a descriptive word to indicate his incompetence as a clergyman.

44. **fain:** gladly; see I. ii. 155.

50. **necessary:** inevitable.

50-1. **knows no end of his goods:** believes his wealth to be endless.

52. **knows no end of them:** is ignorant of them; i.e., is unaware that he is a cuckold; see III. ii. 81.

55. **rascal:** an inferior specimen among deer; the young, lean, or infirm of a herd.

59. **defense:** that is, with the sword or rapier.

62. **dispatch us:** finish us; perform our marriage ceremony.

Philemon and Baucis changed to trees
as Jove's reward for their hospitality.
From Gabriel Simeoni, *La vita et Metamorfoseo d'Ovidio* (1559).

Aud. I am not a slut, though I thank the gods I am foul.

Touch. Well, praised be the gods for thy foulness! Sluttishness may come hereafter. But be it as it may be, I will marry thee; and to that end I have been 40 with Sir Oliver Martext, the vicar of the next village, who hath promised to meet me in this place of the forest and to couple us.

Jaq. [*Aside*] I would fain see this meeting.

Aud. Well, the gods give us joy! 45

Touch. Amen. A man may, if he were of a fearful heart, stagger in this attempt; for here we have no temple but the wood, no assembly but horn-beasts. But what though? Courage! As horns are odious, they are necessary. It is said, "Many a man knows no end of 50 his goods." Right! Many a man has good horns and knows no end of them. Well, that is the dowry of his wife; 'tis none of his own getting. Horns? Even so. Poor men alone? No, no! The noblest deer hath them as huge as the rascal. Is the single man therefore 55 blessed? No; as a walled town is more worthier than a village, so is the forehead of a married man more honorable than the bare brow of a bachelor; and by how much defense is better than no skill, by so much is a horn more precious than to want. 60

Enter *Sir Oliver Martext.*

Here comes Sir Oliver. Sir Oliver Martext, you are well met. Will you dispatch us here under this tree, or shall we go with you to your chapel?

71. **Goddild:** i.e., God yield (reward).

72. **your last company:** that is, on their previous meeting described by Jaques, II. vii. 13 ff.

73-4. **Even a toy in hand here:** I'm just involved in a trivial matter at the moment; **be covered:** put on your hat. Jaques shows the formal courtesy of his day in removing it, probably in satiric acknowledgement of Touchstone's would-be courtly manners.

76. **bow:** part of the yoke. The ox's bow, the horse's curb, and the falcon's bells were used to control them.

81-2. **tell you what marriage is:** give you proper counsel about the responsibilities of marriage and prepare you both more adequately for it.

85. **I am not in the mind but I were:** I am not sure but that I would be.

86. **of:** by.

87. **like:** likely; **well:** Touchstone is punning again. If he marries Audrey he will not be well married in a worldly sense, perhaps, but he does not seriously believe that the marriage will be other than legal.

Oli. Is there none here to give the woman?

Touch. I will not take her on gift of any man.   65

Oli. Truly, she must be given, or the marriage is not lawful.

Jaq. [*Comes forward.*] Proceed, proceed! I'll give her.

Touch. Good even, good Master What-ye-call't.   70
How do you, sir? You are very well met. Goddild you for your last company. I am very glad to see you. Even a toy in hand here, sir. Nay, pray be covered.

Jaq. Will you be married, motley?   75

Touch. As the ox hath his bow, sir, the horse his curb, and the falcon her bells, so man hath his desires; and as pigeons bill, so wedlock would be nibbling.

Jaq. And will you, being a man of your breeding, be married under a bush like a beggar? Get you to   80
church, and have a good priest that can tell you what marriage is. This fellow will but join you together as they join wainscot; then one of you will prove a shrunk panel, and like green timber warp, warp.

Touch. [*Aside*] I am not in the mind but I were   85
better to be married of him than of another; for he is not like to marry me well; and not being well married, it will be a good excuse for me hereafter to leave my wife.

Jaq. Go thou with me and let me counsel thee.   90

Touch. Come, sweet Audrey.
We must be married, or we must live in bawdry.
Farewell, good Master Oliver: not

94-6, 98-100. Touchstone here adapts a popular ballad, commonly known as "Sweet Oliver."

━━━━━━━━━━━━━━━

III. iv. Because Orlando is late for his appointment, Rosalind bewails his unfaithfulness. Corin enters and suggests that there might be sport in watching Silvius woo Phebe; Rosalind is cheered and decides to take a hand in their romance.

━━━━━━━━━━━━━━━

7. **dissembling color:** Judas was traditionally supposed to have had red hair, and red hair also had a traditional connotation of treachery. Rosalind already fears that Orlando is faithless.

> O sweet Oliver,
> O brave Oliver,   95
> Leave me not behind thee!

but

> Wind away,
> Be gone, I say!
> I will not to wedding with thee.   100

[*Exeunt Jaques, Touchstone, and Audrey.*]

Oli. 'Tis no matter. Ne'er a fantastical knave of them all shall flout me out of my calling.

Exit.

Scene IV. [The Forest.]

Enter *Rosalind* and *Celia.*

Ros. Never talk to me! I will weep.

Cel. Do, I prithee; but yet have the grace to consider that tears do not become a man.

Ros. But have I not cause to weep?

Cel. As good cause as one would desire: therefore   5
weep.

Ros. His very hair is of the dissembling color.

Cel. Something browner than Judas's. Marry, his kisses are Judas's own children.

Ros. I' faith, his hair is of a good color.   10

Cel. An excellent color. Your chestnut was ever the only color.

15. **cast lips of Diana:** discarded lips of the goddess who symbolized chastity.

22. **pickpurse:** pickpocket.

24. **concave:** empty, and hence insincere.

29. **tapster:** barkeeper, whose honesty was traditionally questionable.

33. **question:** discourse.

37. **brave verses:** splendid verses. **Brave** is used in more than one sense in this passage, which illustrates the customary Elizabethan love of wordplay. Celia is speaking ironically of Orlando.

39. **traverse:** crosswise; that is, in a devious manner. The point is that Orlando merely fails to turn up instead of announcing frankly that he doesn't want to keep his appointment.

40. **puisny:** an obsolete form of "puny," but in this context meaning "unskillful."

41. **noble goose:** magnificent simpleton.

Ros. And his kissing is as full of sanctity as the touch of holy bread.

Cel. He hath bought a pair of cast lips of Diana. A 15
nun of winter's sisterhood kisses not more religiously;
the very ice of chastity is in them.

Ros. But why did he swear he would come this morning, and comes not?

Cel. Nay, certainly there is no truth in him. 20

Ros. Do you think so?

Cel. Yes. I think he is not a pickpurse nor a horse-stealer; but for his verity in love, I do think him as concave as a covered goblet or a worm-eaten nut.

Ros. Not true in love? 25

Cel. Yes, when he is in; but I think he is not in.

Ros. You have heard him swear downright he was.

Cel. "Was" is not "is." Besides, the oath of a lover is no stronger than the word of a tapster: they are both the confirmer of false reckonings. He attends here in 30
the forest on the Duke your father.

Ros. I met the Duke yesterday and had much question with him. He asked me of what parentage I was. I told him, of as good as he. So he laughed and let me go. But what talk we of fathers when there is 35
such a man as Orlando?

Cel. O, that's a brave man! He writes brave verses, speaks brave words, swears brave oaths, and breaks them bravely, quite traverse, athwart the heart of his lover; as a puisny tilter, that spurs his horse but on 40
one side, breaks his staff like a noble goose. But all's brave that youth mounts and folly guides. Who comes here?

45. **complained of:** sang his lament of love.
50. **pageant:** spectacle.

───────────────────────────────

III. v. Silvius pleads humbly and in vain for a word of kindness from Phebe. Rosalind, indignant at Phebe's cruelty to Silvius, speaks insultingly of her lack of beauty and slight worth. But despite this scorn, Phebe, thinking of course that Rosalind is a handsome boy, falls in love with her. When Rosalind has gone, Phebe sends Silvius with a message to the "tall youth" under the pretext that it is a reply in kind to his scorn.

Enter *Corin.*

Cor. Mistress and master, you have oft enquired
After the shepherd that complained of love,   45
Who you saw sitting by me on the turf,
Praising the proud disdainful shepherdess
That was his mistress.
   Cel.   Well, and what of him?
   Cor. If you will see a pageant truly played   50
Between the pale complexion of true love
And the red glow of scorn and proud disdain,
Go hence a little, and I shall conduct you,
If you will mark it.
   Ros.   O, come, let us remove!   55
The sight of lovers feedeth those in love.
Bring us to this sight, and you shall say
I'll prove a busy actor in their play.

                             Exeunt.

Scene V. [Another part of the Forest.]

Enter *Silvius* and *Phebe.*

Sil. Sweet Phebe, do not scorn me; do not, Phebe!
Say that you love me not, but say not so
In bitterness. The common executioner,
Whose heart the accustomed sight of death makes
    hard,   5

6. Falls: drops.
24. **cicatrice and capable impressure:** visible
impression.

Falls not the axe upon the humbled neck
But first begs pardon. Will you sterner be
Than he that dies and lives by bloody drops?

Enter *Rosalind, Celia,* and *Corin.*

Phe. I would not be thy executioner.
I fly thee, for I would not injure thee.   10
Thou tellst me there is murder in mine eye:
'Tis pretty, sure, and very probable
That eyes, that are the frail'st and softest things,
Who shut their coward gates on atomies,
Should be called tyrants, butchers, murderers!   15
Now I do frown on thee with all my heart;
And if mine eyes can wound, now let them kill thee!
Now counterfeit to swoon; why, now fall down;
Or if thou canst not, O, for shame, for shame,
Lie not, to say mine eyes are murderers!   20
Now show the wound mine eye hath made in thee.
Scratch thee but with a pin, and there remains
Some scar of it; lean but upon a rush,
The cicatrice and capable impressure
Thy palm some moment keeps; but now mine eyes,   25
Which I have darted at thee, hurt thee not,
Nor I am sure there is no force in eyes
That can do hurt.
Sil.   O dear Phebe,
If ever (as that ever may be near)   30
You meet in some fresh cheek the power of fancy,
Then shall you know the wounds invisible
That love's keen arrows make.

43-4. no more . . ./ Than without candle may go dark to bed: no beauty to light up the room. Phebe was a brunet beauty in an age when fairness was the ideal.

47-8. the ordinary/ Of nature's sale-work: the run-of-the-mill production of nature; **'Od's my little life:** God save me.

52. bugle: a black bead.

59. glass: mirror.

60. out of you: that is, because of your flattery.

61. lineaments: features.

Phe.   But till that time
Come thou not near me; and when that time comes,   35
Afflict me with thy mocks, pity me not,
As till that time I shall not pity thee.

  Ros. And why, I pray you? Who might be your
      mother,
That you insult, exult, and all at once,   40
Over the wretched? What though you have no
      beauty—
As, by my faith, I see no more in you
Than without candle may go dark to bed!—
Must you be therefore proud and pitiless?   45
Why, what means this? Why do you look on me?
I see no more in you than in the ordinary
Of nature's sale-work. 'Od's my little life,
I think she means to tangle my eyes too!
No, faith, proud mistress, hope not after it.   50
'Tis not your inky brows, your black silk hair,
Your bugle eyeballs, nor your cheek of cream
That can entame my spirits to your worship.
You foolish shepherd, wherefore do you follow her,
Like foggy south, puffing with wind and rain?   55
You are a thousand times a properer man
Than she a woman. 'Tis such fools as you
That makes the world full of ill-favored children.
'Tis not her glass, but you, that flatters her,
And out of you she sees herself more proper   60
Than any of her lineaments can show her.
But, mistress, know yourself. Down on your knees,
And thank heaven, fasting, for a good man's love;
For I must tell you friendly in your ear,

66. **Cry the man mercy:** beg the man's pardon.

67. **Foul is most foul, being foul to be a scoffer:** physical ugliness is magnified by an ugly disposition.

69. **chide:** scold; **together:** without stopping.

80. **hard:** near.

84. **abused:** deluded.

86. **Dead shepherd:** Christopher Marlowe. The line is from his *Hero and Leander;* **find thy saw of might:** feel the force of your wise saying; see II. vii. 166.

Sell when you can: you are not for all markets.   65
Cry the man mercy, love him, take his offer.
Foul is most foul, being foul to be a scoffer.
So take her to thee, shepherd. Fare you well.

Phe. Sweet youth, I pray you chide a year together.
I had rather hear you chide than this man woo.   70

Ros. He's fall'n in love with your foulness, [*To
Silvius*] and she'll fall in love with my anger. If it be
so, as fast as she answers thee with frowning looks,
I'll sauce her with bitter words.—Why look you so
upon me?   75

Phe. For no ill will I bear you.

Ros. I pray you do not fall in love with me,
For I am falser than vows made in wine.
Besides, I like you not. If you will know my house,
'Tis at the tuft of olives, here hard by.—   80
Will you go, sister?—Shepherd, ply her hard.—
Come, sister.—Shepherdess, look on him better
And be not proud. Though all the world could see,
None could be so abused in sight as he.—
Come, to our flock.   85

                    Exeunt [*Rosalind, Celia,* and *Corin*].

Phe. Dead shepherd, now I find thy saw of might,
"Who ever loved that loved not at first sight?"

Sil. Sweet Phebe—

Phe.   Ha! what sayst thou, Silvius?

Sil. Sweet Phebe, pity me.   90

Phe. Why, I am sorry for thee, gentle Silvius.

Sil. Wherever sorrow is, relief would be.
If you do sorrow at my grief in love,

94-5. By giving love your sorrow and my grief/ Were both extermined: if you would love me, both your sorrow and my grief would be destroyed.

102. erst: once.

107. in such a poverty of grace: so little in your favor.

112-13. erewhile: a while ago.

116. carlot: countryman, cognate with "carl," and "churl."

118. peevish: senseless.

By giving love your sorrow and my grief
Were both extermined. 95
  Phe. Thou hast my love. Is not that neighborly?
  Sil. I would have you.
  Phe.   Why, that were covetousness.
Silvius, the time was that I hated thee,
And yet it is not that I bear thee love; 100
But since that thou canst talk of love so well,
Thy company, which erst was irksome to me,
I will endure; and I'll employ thee too.
But do not look for further recompense
Than thine own gladness that thou art employed. 105
  Sil. So holy and so perfect is my love,
And I in such a poverty of grace,
That I shall think it a most plenteous crop
To glean the broken ears after the man
That the main harvest reaps. Loose now and then 110
A scattered smile, and that I'll live upon.
  Phe. Knowst thou the youth that spoke to me ere-
    while?
  Sil. Not very well, but I have met him oft,
And he hath bought the cottage and the bounds 115
That the old carlot once was master of.
  Phe. Think not I love him, though I ask for him.
'Tis but a peevish boy; yet he talks well.
But what care I for words? Yet words do well
When he that speaks them pleases those that hear. 120
It is a pretty youth—not very pretty—
But sure he's proud; and yet his pride becomes him.
He'll make a proper man. The best thing in him
Is his complexion; and faster than his tongue

131. **constant:** uniform; **mingled damask:** varied in shade like the silk of the same name.

132. **marked:** made note of.

133. **In parcels:** by each separate feature.

139. **remembered:** reminded.

140. **again:** in reply.

141. **omittance is no quittance:** A proverbial expression: That I've neglected to assert myself now does not mean that I may not do so later.

145. **straight:** immediately; see II. i. 74.

146. **matter:** subject matter.

147. **passing short:** very curt.

Did make offense, his eye did heal it up.   125
He is not very tall; yet for his years he's tall.
His leg is but so so; and yet 'tis well.
There was a pretty redness in his lip,
A little riper and more lusty red
Than that mixed in his cheek; 'twas just the difference 130
Betwixt the constant red and mingled damask.
There be some women, Silvius, had they marked him
In parcels as I did, would have gone near
To fall in love with him; but, for my part,
I love him not nor hate him not; and yet   135
I have more cause to hate him than to love him;
For what had he to do to chide at me?
He said mine eyes were black and my hair black;
And, now I am remembered, scorned at me.
I marvel why I answered not again.   140
But that's all one: omittance is no quittance.
I'll write to him a very taunting letter,
And thou shalt bear it. Wilt thou, Silvius?
    Sil. Phebe, with all my heart.
    Phe.   I'll write it straight; 145
The matter's in my head and in my heart.
I will be bitter with him and passing short.
Go with me, Silvius.

                                        Exeunt.

AS YOU LIKE IT

ACT IV

IV. i. Orlando joins Rosalind—an hour late—and receives his first lesson in what he can expect from the caprice of women. Rosalind merrily counsels him that love is not the tragic affair that it is said to be, and that no one ever yet died of the disease. Orlando has promised to join the Duke at dinner but agrees to return in two hours.

▚▚▚▚▚▚▚▚▚▚▚▚▚▚▚▚▚▚▚▚▚▚▚▚

7. **modern censure:** ordinary judgment; see **modern** II. vii. 166.

11. **emulation:** envy; see **emulator,** I. i. 137; **fantastical:** overly fanciful; see III. ii. 401.

13. **politic:** i.e., pretended gravity.

14. **nice:** finical.

16. **simples:** distinct ingredients.

17. **sundry contemplation:** consideration of this and that.

19. **humorous sadness:** fanciful gravity; see I. ii. 269 and II. iii. 9.

ACT IV

Scene I. [The Forest.]

Enter Rosalind *and* Celia *and* Jaques.

Jaq. I prithee, pretty youth, let me be better acquainted with thee.

Ros. They say you are a melancholy fellow.

Jaq. I am so. I do love it better than laughing.

Ros. Those that are in extremity of either are 5
abominable fellows, and betray themselves to every
modern censure worse than drunkards.

Jaq. Why, 'tis good to be sad and say nothing.

Ros. Why then, 'tis good to be a post.

Jaq. I have neither the scholar's melancholy, which 10
is emulation; nor the musician's, which is fantastical;
nor the courtier's, which is proud; nor the soldier's,
which is ambitious; nor the lawyer's, which is politic;
nor the lady's, which is nice; nor the lover's, which is
all these: but it is a melancholy of mine own, com- 15
pounded of many simples, extracted from many objects, and indeed the sundry contemplation of my
travels, in which my often rumination wraps me in a
most humorous sadness.

72

32. **disable:** underrate.
33. **nativity:** birthplace.
36. **gundello:** gondola.

Ros. A traveler! By my faith, you have great reason   20
to be sad. I fear you have sold your own lands to see
other men's. Then to have seen much and to have
nothing is to have rich eyes and poor hands.

Jaq. Yes, I have gained my experience.

Enter *Orlando.*

Ros. And your experience makes you sad. I had   25
rather have a fool to make me merry than experience
to make me sad—and to travel for it too!

Orl. Good day and happiness, dear Rosalind!

Jaq. Nay then, God be wi' you, an you talk in blank
verse!   30

Ros. Farewell, Monsieur Traveler. Look you lisp
and wear strange suits, disable all the benefits of your
own country, be out of love with your nativity and almost chide God for making you that countenance you
are; or I will scarce think you have swam in a   35
gundello. [*Exit Jaques.*] Why, how now, Orlando?
Where have you been all this while? You a lover? An
you serve me such another trick, never come in my
sight more.

Orl. My fair Rosalind, I come within an hour of my   40
promise.

Ros. Break an hour's promise in love? He that will
divide a minute into a thousand parts and break but a
part of the thousandth part of a minute in the affairs
of love, it may be said of him that Cupid hath clapped   45
him o' the shoulder, but I'll warrant him heart-whole.

Orl. Pardon me, dear Rosalind.

49. **of:** by.

52. **jointure:** financial settlement.

63. **leer:** countenance.

70. **graveled:** perplexed.

71. **they are out:** they forget their lines, or are at a loss for words.

73. **shift:** expedient.

Ros. Nay, an you be so tardy, come no more in my
sight. I had as lief be wooed of a snail.

Orl. Of a snail? 50

Ros. Ay, of a snail; for though he comes slowly, he
carries his house on his head—a better jointure, I
think, than you make a woman. Besides, he brings his
destiny with him.

Orl. What's that? 55

Ros. Why, horns, which such as you are fain to be
beholding to your wives for; but he comes armed in
his fortune and prevents the slander of his wife.

Orl. Virtue is no horn-maker, and my Rosalind is
virtuous. 60

Ros. And I am your Rosalind.

Cel. It pleases him to call you so; but he hath a
Rosalind of a better leer than you.

Ros. Come, woo me, woo me, for now I am in a
holiday humor and like enough to consent. What 65
would you say to me now, an I were your very very
Rosalind?

Orl. I would kiss before I spoke.

Ros. Nay, you were better speak first; and when
you were graveled for lack of matter, you might take 70
occasion to kiss. Very good orators, when they are out,
they will spit; and for lovers, lacking (God warn us!)
matter, the cleanliest shift is to kiss.

Orl. How if the kiss be denied?

Ros. Then she puts you to entreaty, and there be- 75
gins new matter.

Orl. Who could be out, being before his beloved
mistress?

91. **in his own person:** i.e., actually, as a real person, not as a character in fiction.

92. **videlicet:** that is to say; **Troilus:** son of King Priam of Troy and lover of Cressida.

95. **Leander:** in Greek legend the lover of Hero, whom he nightly swam the Hellespont to see.

Ros. Marry, that should you, if I were your mistress, or I should think my honesty ranker than my 80
wit.

Orl. What, of my suit?

Ros. Not out of your apparel, and yet out of your
suit. Am not I your Rosalind?

Orl. I take some joy to say you are, because I would 85
be talking of her.

Ros. Well, in her person, I say I will not have you.

Orl. Then, in mine own person, I die.

Ros. No, faith, die by attorney. The poor world is
almost six thousand years old, and in all this time 90
there was not any man died in his own person, videlicet, in a love cause. Troilus had his brains dashed
out with a Grecian club; yet he did what he could to
die before, and he is one of the patterns of love.
Leander, he would have lived many a fair year though 95
Hero had turned nun, if it had not been for a hot midsummer night; for (good youth) he went but forth to
wash him in the Hellespont, and being taken with the
cramp, was drowned; and the foolish chroniclers
of that age found it was "Hero of Sestos." But these 100
are all lies. Men have died from time to time, and
worms have eaten them, but not for love.

Orl. I would not have my right Rosalind of this
mind, for I protest her frown might kill me.

Ros. By this hand, it will not kill a fly! But come, 105
now I will be your Rosalind in a more coming-on disposition, and ask me what you will, I will grant it.

Orl. Then love me, Rosalind.

123. **Go to:** that's enough.
131. **commission:** legal authority.
133. **goes before:** i.e., anticipates.

Ros. Yes, faith, will I, Fridays and Saturdays and all.   110

Orl. And wilt thou have me?

Ros. Ay, and twenty such.

Orl. What sayest thou?

Ros. Are you not good?

Orl. I hope so.   115

Ros. Why then, can one desire too much of a good thing? Come, sister, you shall be the priest and marry us. Give me your hand, Orlando. What do you say, sister?

Orl. Pray thee marry us.   120

Cel. I cannot say the words.

Ros. You must begin, "Will you, Orlando"—

Cel. Go to. Will you, Orlando, have to wife this Rosalind?

Orl. I will.   125

Ros. Ay, but when?

Orl. Why now, as fast as she can marry us.

Ros. Then you must say, "I take thee, Rosalind, for wife."

Orl. I take thee, Rosalind, for wife.   130

Ros. I might ask you for your commission; but I do take thee, Orlando, for my husband. There's a girl goes before the priest, and certainly a woman's thought runs before her actions.

Orl. So do all thoughts; they are winged.   135

Ros. Now tell me how long you would have her after you have possessed her.

Orl. For ever and a day.

Actaeon, and Diana bathing.
From Gabriel Simeoni, *La vita et Metamorfoseo d'Ovidio* (1559).

144. **against rain:** when rain is in the offing.
145. **newfangled:** faddish, attracted by novelty.
147. **Diana in the fountain:** the legend of Actaeon discovering Diana bathing made her a popular subject for garden statuary.
148. **hyen:** hyena.
154. **Make:** close.
159. **Wit, whither wilt:** see I. ii. 53-4.

Ros. Say "a day," without the "ever." No, no, Or-
lando! Men are April when they woo, December 140
when they wed. Maids are May when they are maids,
but the sky changes when they are wives. I will be
more jealous of thee than a Barbary cock-pigeon over
his hen, more clamorous than a parrot against rain,
more newfangled than an ape, more giddy in my de- 145
sires than a monkey. I will weep for nothing, like
Diana in the fountain, and I will do that when you
are disposed to be merry; I will laugh like a hyen, and
that when thou art inclined to sleep.

Orl. But will my Rosalind do so? 150

Ros. By my life, she will do as I do.

Orl. O, but she is wise!

Ros. Or else she could not have the wit to do this.
The wiser, the waywarder. Make the doors upon a
woman's wit, and it will out at the casement; shut 155
that, and 'twill out at the keyhole; stop that, 'twill fly
with the smoke out at the chimney.

Orl. A man that had a wife with such a wit, he
might say, "Wit, whither wilt?"

Ros. Nay, you might keep that check for it till you 160
met your wife's wit going to your neighbor's bed.

Orl. And what wit could wit have to excuse that?

Ros. Marry, to say she came to seek you there. You
shall never take her without her answer unless you
take her without her tongue. O, that woman that can- 165
not make her fault her husband's occasion, let her
never nurse her child herself, for she will breed it like
a fool!

186. **gross:** great; see II. v. 54.
189. **religion:** faith.

Time with a scourge.
From Giovanni Andrea Gilio, *Topica poetica* (1580).

Orl. For these two hours, Rosalind, I will leave
thee.   170

Ros. Alas, dear love, I cannot lack thee two hours!

Orl. I must attend the Duke at dinner. By two
o'clock I will be with thee again.

Ros. Ay, go your ways, go your ways! I knew what
you would prove. My friends told me as much, and I   175
thought no less. That flattering tongue of yours won
me. 'Tis but one cast away, and so, come death! Two
o'clock is your hour?

Orl. Ay, sweet Rosalind.

Ros. By my troth, and in good earnest, and so God   180
mend me, and by all pretty oaths that are not dangerous, if you break one jot of your promise or come
one minute behind your hour, I will think you the
most pathetical break-promise, and the most hollow
lover, and the most unworthy of her you call Rosalind,   185
that may be chosen out of the gross band of the un-
faithful. Therefore beware my censure and keep your
promise.

Orl. With no less religion than if thou wert indeed
my Rosalind. So adieu.   190

Ros. Well, Time is the old justice that examines all
such offenders, and let Time try. Adieu.

                              Exit [*Orlando*].

Cel. You have simply misused our sex in your love-
prate. We must have your doublet and hose plucked
over your head, and show the world what the bird   195
hath done to her own nest.

Ros. O coz, coz, coz, my pretty little coz, that thou

203. **bastard of Venus:** Cupid; that is, the emotion of love.

204. **thought:** melancholy; **spleen:** caprice.

205. **abuses:** deceives; see III. v. 84.

━━━━━━━━━━━━━━━━━━━━━━

IV. ii. Jaques enters with some others of the Duke's company who have killed a deer. They prepare to present it to the Duke triumphantly and sing a song in celebration.

━━━━━━━━━━━━━━━━━━━━━━

3-4. **like a Roman conqueror:** triumphantly.

5. **branch of victory:** laurel garland.

didst know how many fathom deep I am in love! But
it cannot be sounded. My affection hath an unknown
bottom, like the Bay of Portugal.   200

Cel. Or rather, bottomless, that as fast as you pour
affection in, it runs out.

Ros. No, that same wicked bastard of Venus that
was begot of thought, conceived of spleen, and born
of madness, that blind rascally boy that abuses every 205
one's eyes because his own are out—let him be judge
how deep I am in love. I'll tell thee, Aliena, I cannot
be out of the sight of Orlando. I'll go find a shadow,
and sigh till he come.

Cel. And I'll sleep.   210

Exeunt.

Scene II. [The Forest.]

Enter *Jaques,* and *Lords* ([like] *Foresters*)
[with a dead deer].

Jaq. Which is he that killed the deer?

Lord. Sir, it was I.

Jaq. Let's present him to the Duke like a Roman
conqueror; and it would do well to set the deer's
horns upon his head for a branch of victory. Have you 5
no song, forester, for this purpose?

Lord. Yes, sir.

Jaq. Sing it. 'Tis no matter how it be in tune, so it
make noise enough.   *Music.*

S.D. after l. 12. **bear this burden:** sing this refrain.

13. **Take thou no scorn:** don't be ashamed.

|||||||||||||||||||||||||||||||||||||||||||||||||||||||||||||

IV. iii. Orlando is late again and Rosalind is beginning to fret when Silvius delivers Phebe's letter. She reads it aloud to Silvius so that he can see for himself what a fool Phebe is making of him.

Oliver has been seeking Rosalind and Celia to report that Orlando has been wounded in saving him from a hungry lion. Rosalind faints but recovers quickly and pretends that she was merely playing her role as Orlando's mistress. Oliver is skeptical and adjudges Ganymede a puny youth; he and Celia escort her to the sheepcote.

|||||||||||||||||||||||||||||||||||||||||||||

2. **here much Orlando:** here's a lot of Orlando—an ironical comment on his absence.

Song.

What shall he have that killed the deer?   10
His leather skin and horns to wear.
     Then sing him home.
         (*The rest shall bear this burden.*)
Take thou no scorn to wear the horn;
It was a crest ere thou wast born:
     Thy father's father wore it,   15
     And thy father bore it.
The horn, the horn, the lusty horn,
Is not a thing to laugh to scorn.

                            Exeunt.

Scene III. [The Forest.]

Enter *Rosalind* and *Celia*.

Ros. How say you now? Is it not past two o'clock?
and here much Orlando!

Cel. I warrant you, with pure love and troubled
brain, he hath ta'en his bow and arrows, and is gone
forth to sleep.   5

Enter *Silvius*.

Look who comes here.

Sil. My errand is to you, fair youth.
My gentle Phebe bid me give you this.

                       [*Gives a letter.*]

12. **tenure:** tenor.

18. **phoenix:** a bird in legendary lore that existed in only one exemplar. Every five or six hundred years it destroyed itself on a funeral pyre and from its ashes a new phoenix arose; **'Od's my will:** God save me; see III. v. 48.

25. **turned into the extremity of love:** changed into the very essence of love itself.

29. **housewife's hand:** dishpan hands.

A phoenix.
From Geoffrey Whitney, *A Choice of Emblems* (1586).

I know not the contents; but, as I guess
By the stern brow and waspish action   10
Which she did use as she was writing of it,
It bears an angry tenure. Pardon me;
I am but as a guiltless messenger.

Ros. Patience herself would startle at this letter
And play the swaggerer. Bear this, bear all!   15
She says I am not fair, that I lack manners;
She calls me proud, and that she could not love me,
Were man as rare as phoenix. 'Od's my will!
Her love is not the hare that I do hunt.
Why writes she so to me? Well, shepherd, well,   20
This is a letter of your own device.

Sil. No, I protest, I know not the contents.
Phebe did write it.

Ros.   Come, come, you are a fool,
And turned into the extremity of love.   25
I saw her hand. She has a leathern hand,
A freestone-colored hand. I verily did think
That her old gloves were on, but 'twas her hands.
She has a housewife's hand; but that's no matter.
I say she never did invent this letter;   30
This is a man's invention and his hand.

Sil. Sure it is hers.

Ros. Why, 'tis a boisterous and a cruel style,
A style for challengers. Why, she defies me
Like Turk to Christian! Women's gentle brain   35
Could not drop forth such giant-rude invention,
Such Ethiop words, blacker in their effect
Than in their countenance. Will you hear the letter?

52. **eyne:** eyes.

60. **seal up thy mind:** i.e., send a written declaration of your feelings in the matter.

Preparing to open the deer.
The huntsman offers the knife to Queen Elizabeth.
From George Turberville, *The Noble Art of Venery or Hunting* (1575).

Sil. So please you, for I never heard it yet—
Yet heard too much of Phebe's cruelty.   40
  Ros. She Phebes me. Mark how the tyrant writes.
                             Read.

      "Art thou god to shepherd turned,
        That a maiden's heart hath burned?"

Can a woman rail thus?
  Sil. Call you this railing?   45
  Ros.   *Read.*

      "Why, thy godhead laid apart,
        Warrst thou with a woman's heart?"

Did you ever hear such railing?

      "Whiles the eye of man did woo me,
        That could do no vengeance to me."   50

Meaning me a beast.

      "If the scorn of your bright eyne
        Have power to raise such love in mine,
        Alack, in me what strange effect
        Would they work in mild aspect!   55
        Whiles you chid me, I did love;
        How then might your prayers move!
        He that brings this love to thee
        Little knows this love in me;
        And by him seal up thy mind,   60

78. **purlieus:** borders.
80-1. **neighbor bottom:** nearby meadow.
82. **rank of osiers:** line of willows.

Whether that thy youth and kind
Will the faithful offer take
Of me and all that I can make,
Or else by him my love deny,
And then I'll study how to die."   65

Sil. Call you this chiding?

Cel. Alas, poor shepherd!

Ros. Do you pity him? No, he deserves no pity.
Wilt thou love such a woman? What, to make thee an
instrument, and play false strains upon thee? Not to   70
be endured! Well, go your way to her (for I see love
hath made thee a tame snake) and say this to her:
that if she love me, I charge her to love thee; if she
will not, I will never have her unless thou entreat for
her. If you be a true lover, hence, and not a word;   75
for here comes more company.

Exit Silvius.

Enter *Oliver.*

Oli. Good morrow, fair ones. Pray you, if you know,
Where in the purlieus of this forest stands
A sheepcote, fenced about with olive trees?

Cel. West of this place, down in the neighbor bot-   80
   tom.
The rank of osiers by the murmuring stream
Left on your right hand brings you to the place.
But at this hour the house doth keep itself;
There's none within.   85

Oli. If that an eye may profit by a tongue,

89. **female favor:** feminine features.

89-90. **bestows himself/ Like a ripe sister:** conducts himself like a mature woman.

94. **commend him:** send his greetings.

96. **napkin:** handkerchief.

116. **indented glides:** serpentine turnings.

Then should I know you by description—
Such garments and such years: "The boy is fair,
Of female favor, and bestows himself
Like a ripe sister; the woman low,   90
And browner than her brother." Are not you
The owner of the house I did enquire for?

Cel. It is no boast, being asked, to say we are.

Oli. Orlando doth commend him to you both,
And to that youth he calls his Rosalind   95
He sends this bloody napkin. Are you he?

Ros. I am. What must we understand by this?

Oli. Some of my shame, if you will know of me
What man I am, and how, and why, and where
This handkercher was stained.   100

Cel.   I pray you tell it.

Oli. When last the young Orlando parted from you,
He left a promise to return again
Within an hour; and pacing through the forest,
Chewing the food of sweet and bitter fancy,   105
Lo, what befell! He threw his eye aside,
And mark what object did present itself:
Under an oak, whose boughs were mossed with age
And high top bald with dry antiquity,
A wretched ragged man, o'ergrown with hair,   110
Lay sleeping on his back. About his neck
A green and gilded snake had wreathed itself,
Who with her head, nimble in threats, approached
The opening of his mouth; but suddenly,
Seeing Orlando, it unlinked itself   115
And with indented glides did slip away
Into a bush, under which bush's shade

137. **hurtling:** noise, commotion.

148. **our recountments:** the narratives of our fortunes since our parting.

A lioness, with udders all drawn dry,
Lay couching, head on ground, with catlike watch
When that the sleeping man should stir; for 'tis   120
The royal disposition of that beast
To prey on nothing that doth seem as dead.
This seen, Orlando did approach the man
And found it was his brother, his elder brother.

   Cel. O, I have heard him speak of that same 125
     brother,
And he did render him the most unnatural
That lived amongst men.

   Oli.   And well he might so do,
For well I know he was unnatural.   130

   Ros. But, to Orlando! Did he leave him there,
Food to the sucked and hungry lioness?

   Oli. Twice did he turn his back and purposed so;
But kindness, nobler ever than revenge,
And nature, stronger than his just occasion,   135
Made him give battle to the lioness,
Who quickly fell before him; in which hurtling
From miserable slumber I awaked.

   Cel. Are you his brother?

   Ros.   Was it you he rescued?   140

   Cel. Was't you that did so oft contrive to kill him?

   Oli. 'Twas I. But 'tis not I! I do not shame
To tell you what I was, since my conversion
So sweetly tastes, being the thing I am.

   Ros. But, for the bloody napkin?   145

   Oli.   By-and-by.
When from the first to last, betwixt us two,
Tears our recounts had most kindly bathed,

158. **Brief:** in brief.
175. **counterfeited:** pretended.

As how I came into that desert place—
In brief, he led me to the gentle Duke, 150
Who gave me fresh array and entertainment,
Committing me unto my brother's love,
Who led me instantly unto his cave,
There stripped himself, and here upon his arm
The lioness had torn some flesh away, 155
Which all this while had bled; and now he fainted,
And cried, in fainting, upon Rosalind.
Brief, I recovered him, bound up his wound;
And after some small space, being strong at heart,
He sent me hither, stranger as I am, 160
To tell this story, that you might excuse
His broken promise, and to give this napkin,
Dyed in his blood, unto the shepherd youth
That he in sport doth call his Rosalind.

　　　　　　　　　　　[*Rosalind swoons.*]

Cel. Why, how now, Ganymede? sweet Ganymede! 165

Oli. Many will swoon when they do look on blood.

Cel. There is more in it. Cousin Ganymede!

Oli. Look, he recovers.

Ros. I would I were at home.

Cel. We'll lead you thither. I pray you, will you 170
take him by the arm?

Oli. Be of good cheer, youth. You a man? You lack
a man's heart.

Ros. I do so, I confess it. Ah, sirrah, a body would
think this was well counterfeited! I pray you tell your 175
brother how well I counterfeited. Heigh-ho!

Oli. This was not counterfeit. There is too great

178-79. **a passion of earnest:** a genuine fainting.

testimony in your complexion that it was a passion
of earnest.

Ros. Counterfeit, I assure you. 180

Oli. Well then, take a good heart and counterfeit
to be a man.

Ros. So I do; but, i' faith, I should have been a
woman by right.

Cel. Come, you look paler and paler. Pray you draw 185
homewards. Good sir, go with us.

Oli. That will I; for I must bear answer back
How you excuse my brother, Rosalind.

Ros. I shall devise something. But I pray you commend my counterfeiting to him. Will you go? 190

                                    Exeunt.

AS YOU LIKE IT

ACT V

V. i. Audrey protests because Touchstone did not take advantage of the opportunity to have Sir Oliver Martext marry them. William, a former suitor of Audrey, appears and Touchstone puts on his most pompous airs as he warns the bumpkin that Audrey is now his property and his life will be in danger if he does not leave her alone.

⁕⁕⁕⁕⁕⁕⁕⁕⁕⁕⁕⁕⁕⁕⁕⁕⁕⁕⁕⁕⁕⁕

12. **We shall be flouting; we cannot hold:** we cannot help poking fun at people.

From Desiderius Erasmus, *Morias enkomion* (1676).

ACT V

Scene I. [The Forest.]

Enter [*Touchstone the*] *Clown* and *Audrey*.

Touch. We shall find a time, Audrey. Patience, gentle Audrey.

Aud. Faith, the priest was good enough, for all the old gentleman's saying.

Touch. A most wicked Sir Oliver, Audrey, a most 5
vile Martext! But, Audrey, there is a youth here in the forest lays claim to you.

Aud. Ay, I know who 'tis. He hath no interest in me in the world. Here comes the man you mean.

Enter *William.*

Touch. It is meat and drink to me to see a clown. 10
By my troth, we that have good wits have much to answer for. We shall be flouting; we cannot hold.

Will. Good even, Audrey.

Aud. God ye good even, William.

Will. And good even to you, sir. 15

Touch. Good even, gentle friend. Cover thy head,

31-5. **The heathen philosopher . . . open:**
Touchstone's speech in this and the following passage burlesques learned commentary.

cover thy head. Nay, prithee be covered. How old are
you, friend?

Will. Five-and-twenty, sir.

Touch. A ripe age. Is thy name William?   20

Will. William, sir.

Touch. A fair name. Wast born i' the forest here?

Will. Ay, sir, I thank God.

Touch. "Thank God." A good answer. Art rich?

Will. Faith, sir, so so.   25

Touch. "So so" is good, very good, very excellent
good; and yet it is not, it is but so so. Art thou wise?

Will. Ay, sir, I have a pretty wit.

Touch. Why, thou sayst well. I do now remember
a saying, "The fool doth think he is wise, but the wise   30
man knows himself to be a fool." The heathen philosopher, when he had a desire to eat a grape, would
open his lips when he put it into his mouth, meaning
thereby that grapes were made to eat and lips to
open. You do love this maid?   35

Will. I do, sir.

Touch. Give me your hand. Art thou learned?

Will. No, sir.

Touch. Then learn this of me: to have is to have;
for it is a figure in rhetoric that drink, being poured   40
out of a cup into a glass, by filling the one doth empty
the other; for all your writers do consent that *ipse* is
he. Now, you are not *ipse*, for I am he.

Will. Which he, sir?

Touch. He, sir, that must marry this woman. There-   45
fore, you clown, abandon (which is in the vulgar,
leave) the society (which in the boorish is, company)

53-4. I will deal in poison with thee, or in bastinado, or in steel: I will either poison you, beat you with a cudgel, or run you through with sword or dagger; **bandy with thee in faction:** dispute with you as in a political controversy.

54-5. o'errun thee with policy: conquer you by a stratagem.

━━━━━━━━━━━━━━━━━━━━━━━━━━━━

V. ii. To Orlando's surprise, Oliver and Celia have fallen in love at first sight and plan to be married. Oliver is completely reformed and offers his whole estate to Orlando, planning to live as a shepherd in the Forest of Arden. Rosalind is merry at their expense but sobers when Orlando expresses his sorrow that he is still without his Rosalind. She promises by white magic to produce herself for a wedding the next day. Rosalind also promises Silvius and Phebe that she will help to make them happy if they will meet with the others on the morrow.

━━━━━━━━━━━━━━━━━━━━━━━━━━━━

4. persever: accent on the second syllable; the modern word is "persevere."

of this female (which in the common is, woman);
which together is, abandon the society of this female,
or, clown, thou perishest; or, to thy better under-   50
standing, diest; or, to wit, I kill thee, make thee away,
translate thy life into death, thy liberty into bondage.
I will deal in poison with thee, or in bastinado, or in
steel. I will bandy with thee in faction; I will o'errun
thee with policy; I will kill thee a hundred and fifty   55
ways. Therefore tremble and depart.

Aud. Do, good William.

Will. God rest you merry, sir.   *Exit.*

Enter *Corin.*

Cor. Our master and mistress seeks you. Come
away, away!   60

Touch. Trip, Audrey! trip, Audrey! I attend, I attend.

                         Exeunt.

Scene II. [The Forest.]

Enter *Orlando* and *Oliver.*

Orl. Is't possible that on so little acquaintance you
should like her? that but seeing, you should love her?
and loving, woo? and wooing, she should grant? And
will you persever to enjoy her?

Oli. Neither call the giddiness of it in question, the   5

18. **sister:** Oliver has heard of his brother's wooing of Ganymede for Rosalind and addresses her accordingly, since she "brothers" him.

28. **where you are:** i.e., your meaning.

30. **thrasonical:** boastful, like Thraso, a character from Terence's *Eunuchus*.

poverty of her, the small acquaintance, my sudden
wooing, nor her sudden consenting; but say with me,
I love Aliena; say with her that she loves me; consent
with both that we may enjoy each other. It shall be to
your good; for my father's house, and all the revenue 10
that was old Sir Rowland's, will I estate upon you,
and here live and die a shepherd.

Enter *Rosalind.*

Orl. You have my consent. Let your wedding be
tomorrow. Thither will I invite the Duke and all's
contented followers. Go you and prepare Aliena; for 15
look you, here comes my Rosalind.

Ros. God save you, brother.

Oli. And you, fair sister. [*Exit.*]

Ros. O my dear Orlando, how it grieves me to see
thee wear thy heart in a scarf! 20

Orl. It is my arm.

Ros. I thought thy heart had been wounded with
the claws of a lion.

Orl. Wounded it is, but with the eyes of a lady.

Ros. Did your brother tell you how I counterfeited 25
to swoon when he showed me your handkercher?

Orl. Ay, and greater wonders than that.

Ros. O, I know where you are! Nay, 'tis true.
There was never anything so sudden but the fight of
two rams and Cæsar's thrasonical brag of "I came, 30
saw, and overcame." For your brother and my sister
no sooner met but they looked; no sooner looked but
they loved; no sooner loved but they sighed; no

37-8. **incontinent:** a pun: "without delay," and "unchaste."

40. **Clubs:** see *Romeo and Juliet*, I. i. 72, where clubs are one type of weapon called forth to part the brawlers.

52-3. **to some purpose:** all joking aside, earnestly.

53-4. **good conceit:** imagination, intelligence; see II. vi. 8.

55. **insomuch:** because.

58. **grace me:** increase my honor; see I. i. 142.

60. **conversed:** associated.

61. **not damnable:** that is, he practiced only harmless magic and did not deal with the forces of evil.

62. **gesture:** behavior.

sooner sighed but they asked one another the reason;
no sooner knew the reason but they sought the 35
remedy: and in these degrees have they made a pair
of stairs to marriage, which they will climb incontinent, or else be incontinent before marriage. They are
in the very wrath of love, and they will together.
Clubs cannot part them. 40

Orl. They shall be married tomorrow, and I will
bid the Duke to the nuptial. But, O, how bitter a
thing it is to look into happiness through another
man's eyes! By so much the more shall I tomorrow
be at the height of heart-heaviness, by how much I 45
shall think my brother happy in having what he
wishes for.

Ros. Why then, tomorrow I cannot serve your turn
for Rosalind?

Orl. I can live no longer by thinking. 50

Ros. I will weary you then no longer with idle talking. Know of me then (for now I speak to some purpose) that I know you are a gentleman of good
conceit. I speak not this that you should bear a good
opinion of my knowledge, insomuch I say I know you 55
are; neither do I labor for a greater esteem than may
in some little measure draw a belief from you, to do
yourself good, and not to grace me. Believe then, if
you please, that I can do strange things. I have, since
I was three year old, conversed with a magician, most 60
profound in his art and yet not damnable. If you do
love Rosalind so near the heart as your gesture cries
it out, when your brother marries Aliena shall you

66. **inconvenient:** inappropriate.

67. **human as she is:** that is, her human form, not a spirit taking her appearance.

69. **tender dearly:** value exceedingly.

70. **though I say I am a magician:** a confession of dealings in magic was dangerous in view of contemporary statutes condemning practices of witchcraft.

75. **done me much ungentleness:** been most uncivil to me: see uses of **gentle,** I. i. 42 and 158.

77. **It is my study:** that is, I have made a deliberate effort.

78. **despiteful:** spiteful; see **despite,** II. v. 45.

marry her. I know into what straits of fortune she is
driven; and it is not impossible to me, if it appear not 65
inconvenient to you, to set her before your eyes tomorrow human as she is, and without any danger.

Orl. Speakst thou in sober meanings?

Ros. By my life, I do! which I tender dearly,
though I say I am a magician. Therefore put you in 70
your best array, bid your friends; for if you will be
married tomorrow, you shall; and to Rosalind, if you
will.

Enter *Silvius* and *Phebe*.

Look, here comes a lover of mine and a lover of hers.

Phe. Youth, you have done me much ungentleness 75
To show the letter that I writ to you.

Ros. I care not if I have. It is my study
To seem despiteful and ungentle to you.
You are there followed by a faithful shepherd.
Look upon him, love him; he worships you. 80

Phe. Good shepherd, tell this youth what 'tis to
 love.

Sil. It is to be all made of sighs and tears;
And so am I for Phebe.

Phe. And I for Ganymede. 85

Orl. And I for Rosalind.

Ros. And I for no woman.

Sil. It is to be all made of faith and service;
And so am I for Phebe.

Phe. And I for Ganymede. 90

93. **fantasy:** fancy, whimsicality.

95. **observance:** devoted attention; see III. ii. 233.

96. **patience, and impatience:** i.e., **patience** with his mistress's whims, and **impatience** with separations from her.

97. **obedience:** Edmund Malone's conjecture; **observance** is repeated here in the Folios.

111. **Irish wolves:** many parts of Ireland were still in a wild state in Shakespeare's time and wolves were not unknown. The English liked to describe the Irish themselves as "wild."

Orl. And I for Rosalind.

Ros. And I for no woman.

Sil. It is to be all made of fantasy,
All made of passion, and all made of wishes,
All adoration, duty, and observance,   95
All humbleness, all patience, and impatience,
All purity, all trial, all obedience;
And so am I for Phebe.

Phe. And so am I for Ganymede.

Orl. And so am I for Rosalind.   100

Ros. And so am I for no woman.

Phe. [*To Rosalind*] If this be so, why blame you
    me to love you?

Sil. [*To Phebe*] If this be so, why blame you me to
    love you?   105

Orl. If this be so, why blame you me to love you?

Ros. Why do you speak too, "Why blame you me
    to love you?"

Orl. To her that is not here, nor doth not hear.

Ros. Pray you, no more of this; 'tis like the howling 110
of Irish wolves against the moon. [*To Silvius*] I will
help you if I can.—[*To Phebe*] I would love you if I
could.—Tomorrow meet me all together.—[*To Phebe*]
I will marry you if ever I marry woman, and I'll be
married tomorrow.—[*To Orlando*] I will satisfy you if 115
ever I satisfied man, and you shall be married tomorrow.—[*To Silvius*] I will content you if what pleases
you contents you, and you shall be married tomorrow.—[*To Orlando*] As you love Rosalind, meet.—[*To
Silvius*] As you love Phebe, meet.—And as I love no 120

V. iii. Audrey and Touchstone eagerly anticipate their wedding the next day. Two of the Duke's pages come in and sing a merry song about the delights of pastoral love. Touchstone makes fun of them and, as usual, has the better of the repartee.

||||||||||||||||||||||||||||||||||

4. **dishonest:** improper, unmaidenly.

4-5. **a woman of the world:** i.e., a woman who chooses the worldly married state in contrast to the celibate life. Audrey thinks she is marrying into court circles and the phrase has a second meaning referring to the fashionable life she thinks she will lead.

10. **clap into't roundly:** plunge into it briskly.

12. **only:** inevitable.

13. **in a tune:** in the same tune.

13-4. **like two gypsies on a horse:** one of several proverbs may have been in Shakespeare's mind: If two men ride on a horse, one must ride behind; Two of a trade seldom agree; Two sparrows on one ear of corn make an ill agreement.

woman, I'll meet. So fare you well. I have left you commands.

Sil. I'll not fail if I live.

Phe. Nor I.

Orl. Nor I.   125

Exeunt.

Scene III. [The Forest.]

Enter [*Touchstone the*] *Clown* and *Audrey*.

Touch. Tomorrow is the joyful day, Audrey; tomorrow will we be married.

Aud. I do desire it with all my heart; and I hope it is no dishonest desire to desire to be a woman of the world. Here come two of the banished Duke's pages.   5

Enter two *Pages*.

1. Page. Well met, honest gentleman.

Touch. By my troth, well met. Come, sit, sit, and a song!

2. Page. We are for you. Sit i' the middle.

1. Page. Shall we clap into't roundly, without   10 hawking or spitting or saying we are hoarse, which are the only prologues to a bad voice?

2. Page. I' faith, i' faith! and both in a tune, like two gypsies on a horse.

Two Elizabethan pages.
From George Turberville,
The Noble Art of Venery or Hunting (1575).

17. **cornfield:** i.e., wheat field.

18. **In springtime:** the Folios read "In the," though "the" is omitted in the later repeats of the phrase; **the only pretty ring-time:** the best time for marriage.

31. **prime:** spring.

34. **ditty:** verses; **note:** tune; see II. v. 44.

35. **untunable:** untuneful.

Song.

It was a lover and his lass—   15
   With a hey, and a ho, and a hey nonino—
That o'er the green cornfield did pass
   In springtime, the only pretty ring-time,
When birds do sing, hey ding a ding, ding.
Sweet lovers love the spring.   20

Between the acres of the rye—
   With a hey, and a ho, and a hey nonino—
These pretty country folks would lie
   In springtime, &c.

This carol they began that hour—   25
   With a hey, and a ho, and a hey nonino—
How that a life was but a flower
   In springtime, &c.

And therefore take the present time—
   With a hey, and a ho, and a hey nonino—   30
For love is crowned with the prime
   In springtime, &c.

Touch. Truly, young gentlemen, though there was
no great matter in the ditty, yet the note was very
untunable.   35
1. Page. You are deceived, sir. We kept time, we
lost not our time.
Touch. By my troth, yes! I count it but time lost to

V. iv. The several couples meet at the appointed time. The pseudo-Ganymede promises that Rosalind will appear if Orlando wishes to marry her and the Duke will consent. She also exacts a promise from Phebe that she will marry Silvius if she changes her mind about marrying the youth she knows as Ganymede. While the company is awaiting the appearance of Rosalind in her proper form, Touchstone entertains them. Finally Hymen brings in Rosalind and Celia dressed as brides-to-be. Everyone is happily reconciled. In the midst of the nuptial gaiety the third son of Sir Rowland de Boys enters and announces the conversion of Duke Frederick and the restoration of their former estates to the exiles. The play ends with a dance of the happy couples.

━━━━━━━━━━━

4. **fear they hope:** that is, fear that they hope in vain.

6. **urged:** gone over, stated.

hear such a foolish song. God be wi' you, and God
mend your voices! Come, Audrey.   40

> *Exeunt.*

Scene IV. [The Forest.]

Enter *Duke Senior, Amiens, Jaques, Orlando, Oliver,
Celia.*

Duke S. Dost thou believe, Orlando, that the boy
Can do all this that he hath promised?
  Orl. I sometimes do believe, and sometimes do not,
As those that fear they hope, and know they fear.

Enter *Rosalind, Silvius,* and *Phebe.*

  Ros. Patience once more, whiles our compact is   5
    urged.
You say, if I bring in your Rosalind,
You will bestow her on Orlando here?
  Duke S. That would I, had I kingdoms to give with
    her.   10
  Ros. And you say you will have her when I bring
    her?
  Orl. That would I, were I of all kingdoms king.
  Ros. You say you'll marry me, if I be willing?
  Phe. That will I, should I die the hour after.   15
  Ros. But if you do refuse to marry me,
You'll give yourself to this most faithful shepherd?

22. **make all this matter even:** smooth out all difficulties in the way of these plans.

30. **remember:** observe.

31. **lively touches of:** vivid resemblances to; **favor:** appearance; see IV. iii. 89.

36. **desperate:** dangerous.

38. **Obscured:** hidden. The reference to a circle amounts to a pun on the circles used by magicians. See II. v. 57-8.

39. **toward:** in the offing.

Phe. So is the bargain.

Ros. You say that you'll have Phebe, if she will?

Sil. Though to have her and death were both one   20
thing.

Ros. I have promised to make all this matter even.
Keep you your word, O Duke, to give your daughter;
You yours, Orlando, to receive his daughter;
Keep you your word, Phebe, that you'll marry me,   25
Or else, refusing me, to wed this shepherd;
Keep your word, Silvius, that you'll marry her
If she refuse me; and from hence I go,
To make these doubts all even.

                    Exeunt Rosalind and Celia.

Duke..S. I do remember in this shepherd boy   30
Some lively touches of my daughter's favor.

Orl. My lord, the first time that I ever saw him
Methought he was a brother to your daughter.
But, my good lord, this boy is forest-born,
And hath been tutored in the rudiments   35
Of many desperate studies by his uncle,
Whom he reports to be a great magician,
Obscured in the circle of this forest.

Enter [*Touchstone the*] *Clown* and *Audrey.*

Jaq. There is, sure, another flood toward, and these
couples are coming to the ark. Here comes a pair of   40
very strange beasts, which in all tongues are called
fools.

Touch. Salutation and greeting to you all!

Jaq. Good my lord, bid him welcome. This is the

45. **motley-minded:** foolish; see II. vii. 14.

48. **purgation:** trial; see I. iii. 55; **trod a measure:** danced a courtly dance.

49. **politic:** slippery and crafty; see IV. i. 13.

50. **undone:** ruined (by not paying my bills).

51. **like to have fought:** barely escaped fighting.

52. **ta'en up:** made up.

54. **upon the seventh cause:** explained by Touchstone in lines 72-85, 88-90.

58. **Goddild:** God reward; see III. iii. 71; **of the like:** possessed of the like; i.e., the same to you.

60. **copulatives:** couples seeking to be united.

61. **blood breaks:** human impulse breaks the marital vows of fidelity.

65. **your pearl:** pearls in general.

66-7. **swift and sententious:** quick to utter maxims (*sententiae*).

68. **According to the fool's bolt:** "soon shot," as the proverb runs.

69. **dulcet diseases:** pleasant failings. That is, the fault of talking merely to entertain the hearers.

72. **seven times removed:** in the seventh degree of seriousness.

73. **seeming:** seemingly, properly.

motley-minded gentleman that I have so often met in 45
the forest. He hath been a courtier, he swears.

Touch. If any man doubt that, let him put me to
my purgation. I have trod a measure; I have flattered
a lady; I have been politic with my friend, smooth
with mine enemy; I have undone three tailors; I have 50
had four quarrels, and like to have fought one.

Jaq. And how was that ta'en up?

Touch. Faith, we met, and found the quarrel was
upon the seventh cause.

Jaq. How seventh cause? Good my lord, like this 55
fellow.

Duke S. I like him very well.

Touch. Goddild you, sir; I desire you of the like. I
press in here, sir, amongst the rest of the country
copulatives, to swear and to forswear, according as 60
marriage binds and blood breaks. A poor virgin, sir,
an ill-favored thing, sir, but mine own. A poor humor
of mine, sir, to take that that no man else will. Rich
honesty dwells like a miser, sir, in a poor house, as
your pearl in your foul oyster. 65

Duke S. By my faith, he is very swift and sententious.

Touch. According to the fool's bolt, sir, and such
dulcet diseases.

Jaq. But, for the seventh cause. How did you find 70
the quarrel on the seventh cause?

Touch. Upon a lie seven times removed (bear your
body more seeming, Audrey): as thus, sir. I did dis-
like the cut of a certain courtier's beard. He sent me

79. **Modest:** moderate.

80. **disabled:** disqualified, questioned the soundness of; see IV. i. 32.

85. **Circumstantial:** indirect.

90. **measured swords:** checked the respective lengths of our swords, as though about to fight.

91. **nominate:** name.

word, if I said his beard was not cut well, he was in 75
the mind it was. This is called the Retort Courteous.
If I sent him word again it was not well cut, he would
send me word he cut it to please himself. This is
called the Quip Modest. If again, it was not well cut,
he disabled my judgment. This is called the Reply 80
Churlish. If again, it was not well cut, he would
answer I spake not true. This is called the Reproof
Valiant. If again, it was not well cut, he would say I
lie. This is called the Countercheck Quarrelsome and
so to the Lie Circumstantial and the Lie Direct. 85

Jaq. And how oft did you say his beard was not
well cut?

Touch. I durst go no further than the Lie Circumstantial, nor he durst not give me the Lie Direct; and
so we measured swords and parted. 90

Jaq. Can you nominate in order now the degrees of
the lie?

Touch. O sir, we quarrel in print, by the book, as
you have books for good manners. I will name you
the degrees. The first, the Retort Courteous; the sec- 95
ond, the Quip Modest; the third, the Reply Churlish;
the fourth, the Reproof Valiant; the fifth, the Countercheck Quarrelsome; the sixth, the Lie with Cir-
cumstance; the seventh, the Lie Direct. All these you
may avoid but the Lie Direct, and you may avoid that 100
too, with an If. I knew when seven justices could not
take up a quarrel, but when the parties were met
themselves, one of them thought but of an If: as, "If
you said so, then I said so"; and they shook hands and

105. **swore brothers:** took an oath of brotherhood.

109. **stalking horse:** a dummy or covered hiding place used by hunters in stalking game.

110. **presentation:** semblance.

S.D. after l. 110. **Hymen:** in Greek myth the god of marriage; **Still:** soft.

112. **made even:** reconciled; see l. 22.

113. **Atone together:** are made one.

118. **Whose:** that is, Rosalind's.

Hymen, god of marriage.
From Vincenzo Cartari, *Imagini de gli dei de gli antichi* (1609).

swore brothers. Your If is the only peacemaker. Much 105
virtue in If.

Jaq. Is not this a rare fellow, my lord? He's as good
at anything, and yet a fool.

Duke S. He uses his folly like a stalking horse, and
under the presentation of that he shoots his wit.   110

Enter *Hymen, Rosalind,* and *Celia. Still music.*

Hym.   Then is there mirth in heaven
     When earthly things made even
       Atone together.
     Good Duke, receive thy daughter;
     Hymen from heaven brought her,   115
       Yea, brought her hither,
     That thou mightst join her hand with his
     Whose heart within his bosom is.

Ros. To you I give myself, for I am yours.
                              [To Duke]
To you I give myself, for I am yours.   *[To Orlando]*   120
   Duke S. If there be truth in sight, you are my
     daughter.
   Orl. If there be truth in sight, you are my Rosalind.
   Phe. If sight and shape be true,
Why then, my love adieu!   125
   Ros. I'll have no father, if you be not he. *[To Duke]*
I'll have no husband, if you be not he.   *[To Orlando]*
Nor ne'er wed woman, if you be not she.   *[To Phebe]*
   Hym. Peace ho! I bar confusion.
     'Tis I must make conclusion   130

134. **If truth holds true contents:** if faith assures true contentment.

135. **cross:** differences.

139. **sure together:** securely joined.

152. **Even daughter, welcome:** welcome even as a daughter.

Of these most strange events.
Here's eight that must take hands
To join in Hymen's bands,
    If truth holds true contents.
[*To Orlando and Rosalind*]
You and you no cross shall part.   135
[*To Oliver and Celia*]
You and you are heart in heart.
[*To Phebe*]
You to his love must accord,
Or have a woman to your lord.
[*To Touchstone and Audrey*]
You and you are sure together
As the winter to foul weather.   140
Whiles a wedlock hymn we sing,
Feed yourselves with questioning,
That reason wonder may diminish
How thus we met, and these things finish.

Song.

Wedding is great Juno's crown—   145
    O blessed bond of board and bed!
'Tis Hymen peoples every town;
    High wedlock then be honored.
Honor, high honor, and renown
To Hymen, god of every town!   150

Duke S. O my dear niece, welcome thou art to me,
Even daughter, welcome, in no less degree!

161. **Addressed a mighty power:** despatched a large force.

162. **In his own conduct:** under his own command.

171. **engage:** pledge.

173. **offerst fairly to thy brothers' wedding:** give appropriate wedding gifts.

176. **do those ends:** finish those plans.

178. **every:** everyone.

179. **shrewd:** sharp and adverse.

Phe. [*To Silvius*] I will not eat my word, now thou
    art mine;
Thy faith my fancy to thee doth combine.   155

Enter *Second Brother* [*, Jaques de Boys*].

2. Bro. Let me have audience for a word or two.
I am the second son of old Sir Rowland
That bring these tidings to this fair assembly.
Duke Frederick, hearing how that every day
Men of great worth resorted to this forest,   160
Addressed a mighty power, which were on foot
In his own conduct, purposely to take
His brother here and put him to the sword;
And to the skirts of this wild wood he came,
Where, meeting with an old religious man,   165
After some question with him, was converted
Both from his enterprise and from the world,
His crown bequeathing to his banished brother,
And all their lands restored to them again
That were with him exiled. This to be true   170
I do engage my life.
    Duke S.   Welcome, young man.
Thou offerst fairly to thy brothers' wedding:
To one, his lands withheld; and to the other,
A land itself at large, a potent dukedom.   175
First, in this forest let us do those ends
That here were well begun and well begot;
And after, every of this happy number
That have endured shrewd days and nights with us

181. **According to the measure of their states:** each according to his status.

185. **to the measures fall:** begin to dance; see l. 48.

190. **convertites:** converts.

201. **but for two months victualed:** Jaques humorously gibes that their marriage is hardly equipped to last more than two months.

Shall share the good of our returned fortune,   180
According to the measure of their states.
Meantime forget this new-fallen dignity
And fall into our rustic revelry.
Play, music, and you brides and bridegrooms all,
With measure heaped in joy, to the measures fall.   185

  Jaq. Sir, by your patience. If I heard you rightly,
The Duke hath put on a religious life
And thrown into neglect the pompous court.
  2. Bro. He hath.
  Jaq. To him will I. Out of these convertites   190
There is much matter to be heard and learned.
[*To Duke*] You to your former honor I bequeath;
Your patience and your virtue well deserves it.
[*To Orlando*] You to a love that your true faith doth
    merit;   195
[*To Oliver*] You to your land and love and great
    allies;
[*To Silvius*] You to a long and well-deserved bed;
[*To Touchstone*] And you to wrangling, for thy lov-
    ing voyage   200
Is but for two months victualed.—So, to your pleas-
    ures!
I am for other than for dancing measures.
  Duke S. Stay, Jaques, stay.
  Jaq. To see no pastime I! What you would have   205
I'll stay to know at your abandoned cave.   *Exit.*
  Duke S. Proceed, proceed. We will begin these
    rites,
As we do trust they'll end, in true delights.
                      [*The dance begins.*]

[Epilogue.] 2. **unhandsome:** inappropriate.

3-4. **good wine needs no bush:** an allusion to the custom of hanging a bunch of ivy over the door of an alehouse. The custom is lost in antiquity and probably derives from rites relating to Bacchus.

8. **insinuate with you in the behalf of:** slyly influence you in favor of.

9. **furnished:** equipped; see III. ii. 244.

10. **conjure:** plead with you. The accent is on the last syllable.

18. **liked:** pleased.

18-9. **breaths that I defied not:** i.e., breaths that I would risk.

[*Epilogue.*]

Ros. It is not the fashion to see the lady the epilogue; but it is no more unhandsome than to see the lord the prologue. If it be true that good wine needs no bush, 'tis true that a good play needs no epilogue. Yet to good wine they do use good bushes, and good plays prove the better by the help of good epilogues. What a case am I in then, that am neither a good epilogue, nor cannot insinuate with you in the behalf of a good play! I am not furnished like a beggar; therefore to beg will not become me. My way is to conjure you, and I'll begin with the women. I charge you, O women, for the love you bear to men, to like as much of this play as please you; and I charge you, O men, for the love you bear to women (as I perceive by your simp'ring none of you hates them), that between you and the women the play may please. If I were a woman, I would kiss as many of you as had beards that pleased me, complexions that liked me, and breaths that I defied not; and I am sure, as many as have good beards, or good faces, or sweet breaths, will, for my kind offer, when I make curtsy, bid me farewell.

Exeunt.

KEY TO

Famous Lines and Phrases

. . . fleet the time carelessly as they did in the golden
world.   [*Charles*—I. i. 113-14]

. . . I show more mirth than I am mistress of . . .
                             [*Rosalind*—I. ii. 2-3]

. . . the little foolery that wise men have makes a great
show.   [*Celia*—I. ii. 86-7]

Well said! That was laid on with a trowel.
                             [*Celia*—I. ii. 102]

. . . one out of suits with Fortune . . .   [*Rosalind*—I. ii. 245]

Hereafter, in a better world than this,
I shall desire more love and knowledge of you.
                             [*Le Beau*—I. ii. 288-89]

Not one [word] to throw at a dog.   [*Rosalind*—I. iii. 3]

O, how full of briers is this working-day world!
                             [*Rosalind*—I. iii. 11-2]

Beauty provoketh thieves sooner than gold.
                             [*Rosalind*—I. iii. 118]

Sweet are the uses of adversity . . .
                             [*Duke Senior*—II. i. 12]

And this our life, exempt from public haunt,
Finds tongues in trees, books in the running brooks,
Sermons in stones, and good in everything . . .
                             [*Duke Senior*—II. i. 15-7]

. . . He that doth the ravens feed,
Yea, providently caters for the sparrow,
Be comfort to my age!   *[Adam—II. iii. 47-9]*

Though I look old, yet I am strong and lusty;
For in my youth I never did apply
Hot and rebellious liquors in my blood . . .
                              [Adam—II. iii. 51-3]

. . . now am I in Arden, the more fool I! When I was at
     home, I was in a better place; but travelers must be
     content.   *[Touchstone—II. iv. 15-7]*

If thou rememb'rest not the slightest folly
That ever love did make thee run into,
Thou hast not loved.   *[Silvius—II. iv. 33-5]*

[Song] Under the greenwood tree
            Who loves to lie with me . . . *[Amiens—II. v. 1-8]*

I can suck melancholy out of a song as a weasel sucks
     eggs.   *[Jaques—II. v. 11-2]*

[Song] Who doth ambition shun . . . *[All—II. v. 36-43]*

[Song] If it do come to pass
            That any man turn ass . . . *[Jaques—II. v. 48-55]*

A fool, a fool! I met a fool i' the forest . . .
                              [Jaques—II. vii. 13-35]

If ever you have looked on better days . . .
                              [Orlando—II. vii. 121]

All the world's a stage . . .   *[Jaques—II. vii. 149-76]*

[Song] Blow, blow, thou winter wind . . .
                              [Amiens—II. vii. 185-202]

. . . let us make an honorable retreat; though not with bag
     and baggage, yet with scrip and scrippage.
                              [Touchstone—III. ii. 159-61]

O wonderful, wonderful, and most wonderful wonderful!
and yet again wonderful, and after that, out of all
hooping! [*Celia*—III. ii. 191-93]

Dead shepherd, now I find thy saw of might,
"Who ever loved that loved not at first sight?"
[*Phebe*—III. v. 86-7]

Men have died from time to time, and worms have eaten
them, but not for love. [*Rosalind*—IV. i. 101-2]

For ever and a day. [*Orlando*—IV. i. 138]

"Wit, whither wilt?" [*Orlando*—IV. i. 159]

[Song] It was a lover and his lass . . .
[*Pages*—V. iii. 15-32]

A poor virgin, sir, an ill-favored thing, sir, but mine own.*
[*Touchstone*—V. iv. 61-2]

. . . good wine needs no bush . . .
[*Rosalind*—Epilogue 3-4]

---

* Usually misquoted as "A poor thing but mine own."